MODERN PARLIAMENTS

Consulting Editor

NICHOLAS WAHL
Princeton University
COMPARATIVE POLITICS

The Editor

GERHARD LOEWENBERG is Professor of
Political Science at the University of Iowa. He
was awarded his bachelor's, master's, and doc-
toral degrees by Cornell University. Previously
he taught at Mount Holyoke College, and has
been a visiting professor at Columbia, UCLA, and
Cornell. His principal interest in teaching and
research is legislative behavior, particularly in
European political systems. He has spent extensive
periods of time in Great Britain and Germany,
engaged in research supported by a Fulbright
grant and by fellowships from the Rockefeller
Foundation, the Social Science Research Council,
and the Guggenheim Foundation. He is the author
of *Parliament in the German Political System*,
which has also appeared in a revised German
edition. He has contributed to several volumes on
the comparative study of legislatures and political
institutions and has published numerous articles
in scholarly publications.

MODERN

EDITED BY

PARLIAMENTS

CHANGE OR DECLINE?

Gerhard Loewenberg

ALDINE · ATHERTON

Chicago • New York

Modern Parliaments
edited by Gehard Loewenberg

First published 1971 by
Aldine · Atherton, Inc.
529 South Wabash Avenue
Chicago, Illinois 60605

Library of Congress Catalog Number 73–140628
ISBN 202–24075–4, cloth; 202–24103–3, paper

Printed in the United States of America

Preface

The representative assembly, or parliament, as it is most widely called, is at once an old, a ubiquitous, and a controversial political institution. In this century it has attracted the criticism of both disillusioned democrats and true believers in the superior representatives of mass movements or of charismatic leaders. Even among its supporters the institution is incessantly the object of reform.

This volume brings together the views of European and American scholars who share a concern for the vitality of parliament but who differ on what it should be doing and how its performance should be assessed. Writing from the perspective of different national experiences, they display the varied perceptions and expectations of the institution which sustain it even while they make it controversial.

Most of the essays in this volume have not been readily available previously, or have not existed in English. I am grateful to their authors for permission to present them in this context.

Contents

MODERN PARLIAMENTS

The Role of Parliaments in Modern Political Systems

GERHARD LOEWENBERG

Parliament is a paradoxical institution. Medieval in origin, it exists in nearly all contemporary political systems. Although associated with democracy, it has also had its place in aristocracies and dictatorships. Regarded as an ideal instrument of representation, it has at times been composed of instructed as well as autonomous members, who have been variously chosen by birth or appointment as well as by election. The name of the institution derives from *parler,* to talk, yet lawmaking is commonly assumed to be its chief function and talking its main weakness. Although recent research indicates that most parliaments have limited importance in the policy-making process of modern government, few polities, from neighborhood associations to supranational organizations, from long-established to newly independent states, are without this institution. In view of the variety of forms which parliament has taken, the contrasting cultures in which it has appeared, and the tenacity with which it

1

has confounded the prophets of its demise, few generalizations about the institution seem safe.

The very adaptability of parliament makes it a controversial institution. Every stage of its development has attracted criticism from the opponents of change. When the British middle classes used parliament in the seventeenth century to control government policy and expenditure on behalf of their own interests, royalists complained that parliament had exceeded its traditional constitutional role. When representatives of newly enfranchised groups entered European parliaments in the nineteenth century, the established ruling classes regretted the passing of the golden age of the "independent" member. When complex twentieth-century political issues appeared on the agendas of parliaments, and the burden of work moved to specialized committees, observers criticized the declining frequency and quality of great debates on the floor of the House.

The controversies that the institution has attracted through its long history persist to this day. In Great Britain there is a lively dispute over the propriety of specialization among parliamentary committees, in France the constitutional power of parliament in relation to the other institutions of government is unsettled, in Germany there is controversy over the priority which parliament should give to debate on public issues, and in India there is question about the relevance of this medieval European institution to the problems of nation-building in the non-Western world. A self-styled "extraparliamentary opposition" in Western Europe asserts the basic incompatibility of traditional representative assemblies with democracy. Research on legislatures appears to support the view that the institution performs few policy-making functions, but research orientations are themselves controversial.

The essays in this volume give evidence of these contemporary controversies, and they suggest the variety of roles that parliaments are expected to play in modern political systems. They also indicate the widespread existence of the institution, the vastly different forms it takes, and some of the reasons for its remarkable durability.

WHAT IS A PARLIAMENT?

The structure has variously been called parliament, congress, legislature, diet, chamber of deputies, representative assembly, and numerous other terms. No wonder its common features seem elusive. Can even the broadest definition of parliament embrace both a city council of five members and a national assembly of five hundred? An elected chamber like the United States Congress and one in which membership is largely determined by birth, like the British House of Lords? The representative assemblies of predemocratic political systems as well as the democratic chambers in Western Europe and North America today? The Soviets of the USSR as well as the elected houses established in newly independent states? As a matter of fact, all these manifestations of parliament do share at least two identifying structural characteristics, derived from the common ancestry of the institution in medieval Europe: (1) their members are formally equal to one another in status, distinguishing parliaments from hierarchically ordered organizations; and (2) the authority of their members depends on their claim to representing the rest of the community, in some sense of that protean concept, representation.

Certain aspects of the organization and composition of parliaments result from these two structural characteristics. Because of the equality of their status, members of parliament are reluctant to employ sanctions against one another. Parliamentary rules of procedure therefore depend to an extraordinary degree on the implicit folkways of the group, to some extent ponderously registered as precedents, to some extent merely sanctioned by custom and habit. Equality of status also determines that members of parliament work collectively, either in meetings of the entire membership or of committees of members. And concepts of representation affect the composition of parliaments and the roles which their members play.

To be sure, the concept of representation has meant different things to different communities and different generations.[1] It has broadly meant acting for others and binding them, or acting for others and accounting to them; it has meant standing for others on the basis of likeness between the representative and the represented, or on the basis of symbolizing the represented; in modern polities it has been given institutional meaning as the relationship which results from a particular process of selecting the representatives from among the represented. Some of these meanings are compatible, others are mutually exclusive. The specific effects of the concept of representation on the composition and the behavior of parliament depend at any given moment on what the members and their constituents think it means. Some scholars are ready to discard the term because of its ambiguities, yet its age and its accumulation of meanings have made it a potent concept which anyone interested in parliament must conjure with. The various connotations of representation are one source of variance in parliamentary behavior

Although parliament can be defined structurally, it cannot be identified by the particular functions it performs in political systems, for these have varied too widely to have any common denominator. This variety in the activity of the institution explains its extraordinary adaptability to different polities, and its susceptibility to controversy.

THE MODERN CRISES OF PARLIAMENT

To understand the conflicting expectations of parliament which exist today, it is necessary to trace the main stages of its development. Parliament was an old, established political institution before the advent of those characteristics of political systems which we regard as the marks of modernity. It had appeared in thirteenth-century England as an assembly of knights and burgesses summoned irregularly by the monarch in order to consult with him on taxation. In a sense this medieval parliament merely gave new form to those processes of consultation between ruler and ruled which European governments had long used to win acceptance for their policies from the most powerful groups of their subjects. Thus constituted, parliament became the instrument by which newly powerful groups in society could advance their interests. By the end of the seventeenth century, the bourgeoisie had successfully used parliament to secure its political aims, and in doing so, had established the dependence of the monarchy on parliament. Parliament had won the right to sit regularly, to exercise exclusive power to enact legislation and appropriations, and to determine the succession to the throne.

The parliament which had achieved these prerogatives was not a modern institution, however. Its counterparts in western and northern Europe were even more feudal, and less powerful. Each of the characteristics of political modernity—the democratization of the franchise, the surge of political demands generated by urbanization and industrialization, new concepts of political legitimacy—posed challenges to the traditional institution, first in England and soon thereafter in France, Germany, Italy, and the smaller states of Europe. Parliament adapted to all of these challenges, but controversy followed every stage of its modernization.

Democracy

Democracy created the first modern crisis for parliament. With the expansion of the suffrage came political parties to mobilize the new electorate, to recruit representatives from it, and to control these representatives after their election. By the middle of the nineteenth century, observers lamented the disappearance of the "independent" member, the entry of members of new social classes into parliaments, and the control exercised over MPs by the party caucus. In his introduction to the second edition of *The English Constitution,* written five years after the great electoral reform of 1867, Walter Bagehot wondered whether the newly enfranchised masses would show the same deference to "wealth and rank, and to the higher qualities of which these are the rough symbols and common accompaniments," which he regarded as a prerequisite of parliamentary government.[2] A generation later Ostrogorski described the threat of the extraparliamentary party caucus to the independence of members of parliament, and Sidney Low as well as A. Lawrence Lowell raised alarms about the pernicious influence of party discipline within the House of Commons.[3]

Recent research indicates that behind the appearance of the independence of members of parliament in the nineteenth century there existed sectional and economic interests which determined parliamentary voting behavior. Those MPs who were independent of their party leaders were usually acting on behalf of these special interests.[4] But the writers of the most prominent analyses of the nineteenth-century parliament were so blinded by their aristocratic biases that they could not see the influence of vested interests in the predemocratic House of Commons. Noting only the absence of strict party organization, they concluded that the members were independent, moved only by conscience. Impressed also by the educational level of members at that time, and by the eloquence evident in debate, these authors established the myth of the golden age of parliament, which became the standard for measuring its subsequent decline.

In his *Modern Democracies,* published in 1921, Lord Bryce gave influential expression to this view. He noted the evil effects of party machines in the United States, of unstable and warring groups in the French chamber, of party discipline in Great Britain, and of the changing class composition of parliaments on their deliberative style everywhere. He perceived the mounting importance of interest groups as forums for political discussion in competition with parliament, and the growing complexity of the issues with which parliament had to deal. He concluded that representative assemblies were losing authority to the executive and to the electorate.[5] Writing just after the First World War, Bryce at once summarized the view of an entire generation of observers of representative institutions and provided a dogma for a new generation of disillusioned democrats. To this day, it is part of the conventional wisdom about parliaments to regard the influence of parties as pernicious.

Specialization

If the expansion of the suffrage transformed the composition of parliament and the distribution of influence among its members, the expansion of demands made on government by newly industrialized and urbanized societies transformed the pattern of parliamentary activity and created the second crisis of the institution. Some parliaments responded to the growing burden of lawmaking and the increasing complexity of the issues by adopting a division of labor among their members which constituted at least a pale imitation of bureaucratic organization. Although committees of parliament had long existed, the development of specialized standing committees was a product of the late nineteenth century and occurred particularly in those parliaments which were free of executive domination. In France and Germany, for example, specialized committees flourished, while in Great Britain successive Governments steadfastly opposed them. As John P. Mackintosh explains, the modern party system gave the prime minister and his colleagues such control over their followers in Parliament that "the Commons became reduced to registering the results of general elections and to passing virtually all the legislation put before it." Governments realized that specialized committees in the House of Commons "would be an extra source of pressure on ministers." They did not want to yield their power over the House, nor could they be compelled to do so.[6]

However, as Mackintosh writes, "whenever it was felt that the House was definitely failing to discharge one of its major functions, the device of a committee was adopted." To scrutinize government expenditure, the House of Commons has had a Public Accounts Committee since 1861 and, intermittently since 1912, a Committee on Estimates. In 1944 the House established a committee to supervise delegated legislation, and in 1956 one on the nationalized industries. But the broadest attempt to employ specialized committees to increase the capacity of Parliament to deal with complex policy issues occurred in the House of Commons elected in 1966.

Mackintosh describes how the Labor Government at that time agreed to experiment with a series of specialized committees, under the influence of some of its leaders who had academic commitments to parliamentary reform and some of its youngest and ablest backbenchers, who exhibited the unusually critical attitude toward British institutions characteristic of their generation. Mackintosh, as a member of this backbenchers' group, experienced the hopes and disappointments associated with the establishment of the new committees. In his essay in this volume (pp. 33–63) he analyzes the prospects which these committees have of increasing the influence of members of parliament over Government policy, and he also reveals the obstacles which the committees have encountered under the British system of cabinet government. Whatever the results of the experiment, it is clear that some increase in specialization is on the agenda of parliamentary reform in Great Britain in the 1970s.

By curious contrast, continental European parliaments have been reacting against a level of specialization which had developed earlier and had gone further. Under the French Fourth Republic, nineteen specialized committees of the National Assembly had exercised enormous influence over legislation, entirely free of Government control. Among the many restrictions which the constitution of the Fifth French Republic imposed upon the Assembly in 1958, one limited the number of parliamentary committees to six and another curtailed the power of committees in the legislative process.[7] Similarly, in postwar Germany, the Bundestag had established over forty committees in its first term, each having jurisdiction within a narrow policy area. Both the magnitude and the complexity of the political issues at that time, as well as the desire of interest groups to have parliamentary committees corresponding to their precise area of concern, produced this proliferation. By 1957, the problem of coordination among all of these committees had become so great, and the Government had found them so unmanageable, that their number was reduced to twenty-six. Two further reductions left seventeen specialized standing committees and two specialized ad hoc committees in existence in the Bundestag at the start of the 1970s.

Parliamentary reformers in Germany were generally concerned with what they regarded as excessive specialization and bureaucratization, manifesting itself in the emphasis which members of the Bundestag placed on the scrutiny of the details of legislation in the privacy of legislative committees. By the standard of the British parliament, which German scholars have frequently regarded as the parliamentary ideal, the Bundestag neglected open debate of the great public issues. The tradition of great parliamentary debates as the focal point of public political attention never developed in Germany as it had in Great Britain. The combative and ideological environment in which the German parliament developed at the end of the nineteenth century was not conducive either to extemporaneous speech or to the prospect of verbal persuasion.[8] More recently, the appearance of new media of communication between political leaders and their constituents—party conferences, press briefings, television addresses—detracted from the parliamentary forum. Despite these traditional and contemporary obstacles to the performance of a debating function by the Bundestag, promotion of public debate continues to be a major objective of parliamentary reform in Germany. Walter Bagehot's famous enumeration of the expressive, teaching, and informing function of parliament, and his assertion of the priority of these functions over lawmaking, is frequently quoted with approval.[9] Wilhelm Hennis, writing in this reformist tradition, declares that "what parliament accomplishes in its committees . . . could also be done by other institutions."[10] The distinctive activity of parliament, Hennis says, "takes place on the floor of the House. . . ." He explains the purposes of parliamentary debate, admonishes the parties for neglecting it, and implies that the electorate must ultimately demand governmental accountability in the forum of parliament.

Some reforms intended to enliven debate were in fact undertaken by the Bundestag during the 1960s. The use of oral questions was encouraged, brief debates on current issues in the style of the British adjournment debates were instituted, a time limit was set for individual speakers, television coverage of debate was permitted, committees held a growing number of open hearings, and proposals were made to rebuild the chamber of the Bundestag to emulate the informality and intimacy of the House of Commons. Despite these changes, however, the Bundestag continued to meet in public sessions far less often than other Western European parliaments and a preponderance of its work continued to be done in closed committee meetings. Furthermore, while some reforms sought to promote debate, others concentrated on improving the Bundestag's sources of information and on augmenting its staff. In view of the complexity and the volume of issues facing members of parliament, it seemed necessary to take steps to match the expertise available to the ministries. In this way specialization was encouraged in another form. According to Hennis, this introduced a new diversion from parliament's essential function.

Thus, the issue of specialization was seen differently in Great Britain, where the House of Commons was only beginning to approach specialization, from the way it was regarded in Germany and France, where parliamentary specialization had gone very far.

Executive-Legislative Relationships

On the question of parliamentary power, however, there was a different alignment among these three states. The objective of parliamentary reform in Great Britain and Germany was to increase the power of parliament in relationship to the executive. Under the influence of repeated warnings of the decline of parliament, all reforms advocated in England—including committee specialization—sought to strengthen the institution. In Germany, vivid memories of the virtual collapse of the Reichstag in 1930 and the association of its demise with the advent of Nazism led to the conviction that democracy depended on the vitality of parliament. In France, however, the object of reform was different. Long years of "assembly government" under the Third and Fourth Republics, when parliamentary power was accompanied by governmental weakness, caused reformers to address themselves to reversing what was perceived to be the Assembly's dominance. Michel Debré, the main author of the constitution of the Fifth Republic, moved in this direction when he drafted the provisions which circumscribed the power of the French parliament in 1958.

As François Goguel explains, in the 1950s "it was obvious to all that the disordered state of the French political system was due to the existence of the practically unlimited sovereignty of Parliament." For this reason, there was very wide support in 1958 for a regime which, according to Goguel, "provided for a better division of labor between Government and Parliament, that is to say, a limitation of parliamentary power, while maintaining the fundamental principle of a parliamentary system, that of the political responsibility of the Government to the National Assembly."[11] If, after a decade of experience under the new regime, parliament seemed threatened by executive domination, Goguel regards this as a failure of the National Assembly to adapt itself to its new constitutional position.

Philip Williams, however, criticizes the executive for insisting on its new powers to an extent inconsistent with the operation of parliamentary government. "First the Government took for itself a formidable arsenal of [constitutional] powers to serve as a substitute for a majority," Williams writes, but after the Gaullists unexpectedly acquired a majority, the Government took "full advantage of both its political and procedural strength. . . ."[12] The difference in outlook between Goguel and Williams reflects the long-standing controversy about the proper role of parlia-

ment in the French political system. This controversy is stimulated by the variety of the French experience in the twentieth
century, which has included sharp fluctuations between parliamentary dominance under the Third Republic until 1940, executive dominance under the Vichy regime after the defeat of
France, the restoration of parliamentary supremacy under the
Fourth Republic in 1946, and the ascendance of the executive
under de Gaulle between 1958 and 1969. The retirement of de
Gaulle at the end of that decade threatened the cohesion of the
Government's majority in the National Assembly and created
new possibilities for changing the executive-legislative balance.

If the advent of democracy and modern political parties posed
the first crisis of the modern parliament, and the rising level of
political demand with its tendency toward specialization posed
the second, the appearance of plebiscitary leadership and executive domination posed the third crisis. Just after Bryce wrote in
1921, this type of dictatorship overwhelmed the Italian parliament, as it was to do a decade later in Germany. These two dramatic assertions of executive domination were subsequently repeated in other states. It seemed as if parliament, once the
uniquely representative institution in the modern system of government, was being displaced by executives capable of justifying
their authority by new concepts of representation. With the use
of referenda, plebiscitary elections, and ideological parties, a succession of leaders gained ascendance over both old and new parliaments in Italy and Germany, in Spain and France, in some of
the old states of Eastern Europe, and in some of the newly independent states of Asia and Africa. Yet in many of these cases
parliaments survived and reasserted themselves, or were restored. When the authority of plebiscitary leaders proved difficult
to transmit to their successors, there was a return to leadership
recruited by parliament. When dominant executives ignored
powerful interests existing in the community, these were articu-
lated and pressed in parliament. When the personification of the
state in a particular leader lost its magic, there was a reversion to

the symbols of legitimacy provided by parliament. The replacements of parliament by popularly endorsed leaders, which were such frequent occurrences between 1920 and 1960, seem in retrospect to be exceptional events, reflecting interval regimes rather than long-term institutional change.

Effects of Political Modernization

The existence of parliament as an institution of government is particularly remarkable in the newly independent states in which it lacks organic roots and is frequently the product of colonial rule. Yet parliament appears capable of contributing to the integration of new nations as it once played a part in nation-building in Europe. Henry C. Hart has examined this function of parliament by comparing the role of parliament in England in the mid-eighteenth century with its role in India in the two decades since independence. In both cases Hart finds parliament regulating the recruitment of executive leaders, unifying the nation, linking interest groups to government, and incubating an opposition.[13] Despite the difficulties of comparing the processes of politics at two very different points in time, such diachronic comparison does suggest why a political institution which originated in medieval Europe has survived its colonial sponsors in parts of Asia and Africa.

The proliferation of nation-states in the twentieth century has brought with it a proliferation of parliaments. A similar result appears likely as a consequence of the search for new levels of decision-making both above and below the nation-state. The regional councils established in France since 1966, with planning authority for a city as well as its surrounding suburbs, are examples of new subnational assemblies. The European Parliament illustrates the development at the supranational level. Both types of assemblies may play a significant role in the creation of new levels of political community, parallel to the role of national parliaments in nation-building. Whether or not this expectation is realized, the appearance of parliament in new polities indicates that it still attracts the hopes of constitution-makers despite the disillusionment of many of its critics.

In the process of political modernization, parliament seems to have experienced the fate of many premodern institutions. Typically, political development brings a multiplication of political structures, each more specialized than the multifunctional institutions of the old regime.[14] Parliament, originally a consultative body for monarchs, then a body declaring the law and registering grievances, has increasingly faced competition from more specialized consultative, lawmaking, and adjudicative agencies. Experts in the civil service exercise much of the legislative initiative today, interest groups provide direct consultative links between specialized publics and the relevant government departments, and mass media give political leaders direct access to the whole citizenry. This does not mean that parliament has ceased to perform policy-making or communications functions but rather that it now shares these functions with newer institutions.

With the advent of democracy and the declining legitimacy of monarchy as an agency of government in the late nineteenth century, two functions of parliament acquired a new importance: the selection of cabinet ministers and the legitimation of policy. In most Western European states early in this century, the executive consisted of a prime minister and his cabinet selected from among the leaders of the majority party or parties in parliament and dependent for their democratic legitimation on the continuing confidence of the people's representatives in the elected House. But even in the performance of the functions of recruitment and legitimation, parliament soon faced competition from processes of direct presidential election and popular referendum which appeared to give the people the capacity to bestow democratic legitimacy on government without the intermediary activity of parliament. In Weimar Germany between 1919 and 1933, in Gaullist France after 1958, and among the leaders of the "extraparliamentary opposition" which appeared in many Western European states in the 1960s, the preference for a more direct form of democracy than that afforded by parliamentary representation has sporadically challenged parliament's role in selecting the head of government and enacting policy.

Because it is not a functionally specific institution, parliament has exhibited a remarkable flexibility in adapting to the changes imposed by political modernization. In the process, it has lost its monopoly in the performance of major political functions, sharing these now with newer agencies and processes. Nevertheless, few political systems have found the institution expendable.

CONTROVERSIES IN THE ASSESSMENT OF PARLIAMENTS

The long history of parliament helps to explain the conflicting expectations of the institution which have caused successive generations of observers to conclude that representative assemblies were declining in quality and in political importance. Such judgments were often the result of applying the standards of a previous stage of institutional development to the parliamentary behavior of the moment. Late-nineteenth-century criticism of democratically elected parliaments, for example, applied standards of eloquence in debate, courtesy among members, and independence of party which were derived from the bourgeois, oligarchical parliaments of the eighteenth century. Twentieth-century criticism of specialized, committee-ridden parliaments used standards derived from nineteenth-century parliaments operating in political systems of limited scope. Criticism of the parliaments of newly independent states compares them to long-standing parliaments in highly developed systems rather than to parliaments during the nation-building stages of Western political history. Decline, in short, is in the eye of the beholder and depends on his analytical perspectives.

The academic study of legislatures has long been influenced by an eighteenth-century model of the political system, a model which regards the legislature as the central policy-making institution that Anglo-American constitutional lawyers in the seventeenth and eighteenth centuries expected it to be. This is a demand-input model of representative institutions which assumes that citizens have well-formulated policy preferences and that the function of the members of the representative assembly is to convert these preferences into public policies. The study of public opinion and legislative behavior within the last two decades, however, has discovered strong evidence that neither of these assumptions is tenable. John C. Wahlke has summarized the research conclusions which show that the public does not have clear policy preferences and that legislators do not reach their decisions in response to public demands.[15] There is little reason to believe that they ever did. The demand-input model may have justified the claim of the legislature to policy-making power in the political system, but its assumptions have little empirical basis.

If legislative behavior is evaluated in terms of this conception of politics, performance naturally falls short of expectations. Furthermore, the standards of the demand-input model are equally unrealistic for measuring the behavior of other representative institutions. The question, then, is whether the standards or the institutions are to blame.

Wahlke concludes that it "is not . . . that representative democracy is chimerical but . . . that our conceptions of . . . representation are somehow deficient." He believes that in focusing on the policy-making functions of the legislature we have overlooked its larger impact on the stability of the political system. Wahlke therefore suggests that representative assemblies be regarded as part of the "support" rather than the "demand mechanism" of the political system, a proposal which would turn attention to some of the earliest functions of parliament, those of sustaining authority and building political community.

The growing body of research on legislative behavior during the 1950s and 1960s chiefly tried to explain the decisions of representative assemblies in terms of the interest groups, parties, and constituencies which made demands on them. Wahlke suggests that we use this knowledge of legislative behavior to explain larger attributes of the political system. In view of the proliferation of parliaments and the historical record of some of the older parliaments, a large amount of data is available for comparative analysis. Comparisons of parliaments at various political levels and at different points in time, as well as cross-national comparisons at one point in time, permit us to examine a wide range of variance in parliamentary behavior. If this variance can be related to such system characteristics as political stability, scope of politics, and style of leadership, we may arrive at a new assessment of parliament.

Empirical research thus promises more reliable answers than we have ever had to questions about what parliaments do in modern political systems. Controversies about what parliaments ought to do will nevertheless continue among those having conflicting normative expectations of this institution.

Half a century after Bryce's observations on the decline of the legislature, the institution experienced a particularly basic challenge. The political crises of the 1960s and 1970s called the desirability of representation itself into question, reviving the old controversy between the advocates of direct and representative democracy. In this controversy, for once, parliament was attacked not for adapting itself to unwelcome political changes but for being fundamentally incapable of responding to the urgent needs of a democratic society. In their condemnations of representative assemblies, the proponents of more direct forms of political action echoed Rousseau's noted critique of representation. Writing in the time of the unreformed House of Commons, Rousseau had declared:

> Sovereignty cannot be represented, for the same reason that it cannot be alienated. It consists essentially of the general will, and will cannot be represented. Either it is itself or it is different. There is no middle term. The Deputies of the People are not, nor can they be, its representatives. They can only be its Commissioners. They can make no definite decisions. Laws which the people have not ratified in their own person are null and void. That

is to say, they are not laws at all. The English people think they are free, but in this belief they are profoundly wrong. They are free only when they are electing members of Parliament. Once the election has been completed, they revert to a condition of slavery: they are nothing. Making such use of it in the few short moments of their freedom, they deserve to lose it.[16]

Direct democracy received institutional expression long ago in the Swiss communes which Rousseau admired and in the town meetings of New England, which have had no similarly distinguished exponent. In larger polities the plebiscite and the referendum have provided means by which voters could act directly on policy questions, although the consistency of these devices with other democratic institutions has been uncertain. In France, the Napoleonic use of plebiscite and referendum early gave them an authoritarian taint, which de Gaulle's recent resurrection of these procedures hardly erased.[17] Elsewhere in Western Europe, where referenda have been occasionally employed, their use has always aroused the suspicion of democrats; they have never been used in Great Britain or in most of the older parliamentary systems. In the United States, the initiative and the referendum were favorite instruments of early twentieth-century reformers anxious to bypass the political bosses, but in practice they have been neither as popular nor as effective as their proponents had hoped.

Direct democracy has often been the resort of men impatient with the performance of representative assemblies, distrustful of their responsiveness to what is believed to be the popular will, or romantically attached to the value of direct participation. It is not surprising, therefore, that the political crises of the 1960s and 1970s in Europe and the United States reawakened the old controversy between direct and representative democracy or that parliament as the most prominent representative institution should be the object of a new critique. The members of the "extraparliamentary opposition" which appeared in Germany, France, and Italy, and their counterparts in the United States, shared a set of preferences about political action based on a fundamental distrust of representation. They preferred open confrontation between adversaries to deliberation between their agents, expression of views by public demonstration to transmission of beliefs through established procedures, direct community action to constituency influence on regular officeholders, and substantive to procedural legitimacy. Each of these preferences challenged premises underlying representative assemblies: that the people are too numerous to make policy decisions, that their representatives can act on behalf of their interests, that parliamentary procedures facilitate decision-making, that the legitimacy of a decision depends on the manner in which it is made. The new advocates of direct democracy doubted that parliaments could be instruments of the popular will, capable of dealing systematically with complex social problems and reaching morally justifiable decisions. They believed that representative assemblies could not ultimately escape their predemocratic origins.

Thus parliament continues to attract lively controversy. There is disagreement about what it does and what difference it makes, about what it ought to do and what it can do. A strong revival of scholarly interest in legislatures may help to resolve the first two disagreements, but differences over political values assure the persistence of the last two. Meanwhile, repeated prophecies of the demise of parliament have proven to be premature if not clearly mistaken. Old parliaments survive and new ones are constantly established. The institution seems to be one of the most enduring and widely applicable inventions of political man.

NOTES

1. See Hanna Fenichel Pitkin, ed., *Representation* (New York: Atherton Press, 1969).
2. Walter Bagehot, *The English Constitution* (Ithaca, N.Y.: Cornell University Press, 1966), p. 272.

3. M. Ostrogorski, *Democracy and the Organization of Political Parties* (London: Macmillan, 1902); Sidney Low, *The Governance of England* (London: T. Fisher Unwin, 1904); A. Lawrence Lowell, *The Government of England* (New York: Macmillan, 1920), chapter 35.

4. Hugh Berrington, "Partisanship and Dissidence in the Nineteenth-Century House of Commons," *Parliamentary Affairs,* XXI (1968), 338–374.

5. Chapter 1 of this volume, "The Decline of Legislatures," below.

6. This and the following quotations are from chapter 2 of this volume.

7. Constitution of the Fifth French Republic, articles 42 and 43.

8. Ernst Fraenkel, "Historische Vorbelastungen des deutschen Parlamentarismus," *Vierteljahreshefte für Zeitgeschichte,* VIII (1960), 333.

9. Walter Bagehot, *The English Constitution,* chapter IV.

10. This and the following quotations are from chapter 3 of this volume.

11. Chapter 4 of this volume.

12. Chapter 5 of this volume.

13. Chapter 6 of this volume.

14. Gabriel A. Almond and G. Bingham Powell, Jr., *Comparative Politics: A Developmental Approach* (Boston: Little, Brown, 1966), chapter XI.

15. Chapter 7 of this volume.

16. *Social Contract,* Book III, chapter 15.

17. Henry W. Ehrmann, "Direct Democracy in France," *The American Political Science Review,* LVII (December 1963), 883–901.

1

The Decline of Legislatures

JAMES BRYCE

In Modern Democracies, *the two-volume work from which the following selection is taken, the British historian and statesman James Bryce (1838–1922) formulated generalizations about democratic government based on his observation of the democratic states of his time. The book is one of the first texts in comparative politics, scientific up to a point yet implicitly accepting nineteenth-century British government as the standard for evaluating other political systems. Bryce, who had served in the House of Commons, examined the effect of modern political parties and universal suffrage on parliament and found the result dismaying. His influential analysis of the decline of legislatures has colored the view of observers on both sides of the Atlantic to this day. Although the actual behavior of the nineteenth-century House of Commons has not been carefully studied, the notion that this was the golden age of parliament has been widely accepted, with remarkably little concern about using an essentially predemocratic parliament as a model for evaluating contemporary legislatures.*

I

Every traveler who, curious in political affairs, inquires in the countries which he visits how their legislative bodies are work-

Reprinted with the permission of The Macmillan Company (New York) and Macmillan & Co. Ltd. (London) from James Bryce, *Modern Democracies* (New York: Macmillan, 1921). Copyright 1921 by The Macmillan Company; renewed 1949 by Margaret Vincentia Bryce, Roland L'Estrange Bryce, and Rosalind L'Estrange Tudor Craig.

21

ing, receives from the elder men the same discouraging answer. They tell him, in terms much the same everywhere, that there is less brilliant speaking than in the days of their own youth, that the tone of manners has declined, that the best citizens are less disposed to enter the Chamber, that its proceedings are less fully reported and excite less interest, that a seat in it confers less social status, and that, for one reason or another, the respect felt for it has waned. The wary traveler discounts these jeremiads, conscious of the tendency in himself, growing with his years, to dwell in memory chiefly upon the things he used to most enjoy in his boyhood—the long fine summers when one could swim daily in the river and apples were plentiful, the fine hard winters when the ice sheets on Windermere or Loch Lomond gathered crowds of skaters. Nevertheless this disparagement of the legislatures of our own day is too general, and appears in too many forms, to be passed by. There is evidence to indicate in nearly every country some decline from that admiration of and confidence in the system of representative government which in England possessed the generation who took their constitutional history from Hallam and Macaulay, and their political philosophy from John Stuart Mill and Walter Bagehot; and in the United States that earlier generation which between 1820 and 1850 looked on the Federal System and the legislatures working under it in the nation and the States as the almost perfect model of what constitutional government ought to be.

In the middle of the last century most Liberal thinkers in France and Spain, in Italy and Germany expected a sort of millennium from the establishment in their midst of representative institutions like those of England, the greatest improvement it was often said, that had ever been introduced into government, and one which, had the ancient world discovered it, might have saved the Greek republics from the Macedonian conqueror and Rome from the despotism of the Caesars. So the leaders of the revolutions which liberated Spanish America took as their pattern the American Federal System which had made it possible for a central Congress and legislative bodies in every State to give effect to the will of a free people scattered over a vast continent, holding them together in one great body while also enabling each division of the population to enact laws appropriate to their respective needs. By the representative system the executive would, they believed, be duly guided and controlled, by it the best wisdom of the country would be gathered into deliberative bodies whose debates would enlighten the people, and in which men fit for leadership could show their powers. Whoever now looks back to read the speeches and writings of statesmen and students between 1830 and 1870, comparing them with the complaints and criticisms directed against the legislatures of the twentieth century, will be struck by the contrast, noting how many of the defects now visible in representative government were then unforeseen.

These complaints and criticisms need to be stated and examined, if only in view of the efforts which peoples delivered from the sway of decadent monarchies, are now making to establish constitutional governments in various parts of Central and Eastern Europe. . . .

II

In the States of the American Union a sense of these failings has led to two significant changes. Many restrictions have been everywhere imposed by constitutional amendments on the powers of State legislatures; and more recently many States (nearly one-third of the whole number) have introduced the Referendum and the Initiative, the former to review, the latter from time to time to supersede the action of those bodies. The virtue of members had so often succumbed to temptations proceeding from powerful incorporated companies, and the habit of effecting jobs for local interests was so common, that a general suspicion had attached itself to their action. Moreover, the so-called "Party Machines," which have been wont to nominate candidates, and on whose pleasure depends the political future of a large proportion of the members, prevented the will of the people from prevailing, making many members feel themselves responsible rather to it than to their constituencies. Like faults have been sometimes charged against Congress, though conditions are better there than in most of the States, but the Referendum and Initiative are of course inapplicable to the National government since the Federal Constitution makes no provision for them.

In France, while Paris is enlivened, the nation has been for many years wearied by the incessant warfare of the Chamber, divided into many unstable groups, with frequent changes from one Cabinet to another. The politicians have become discredited, partly by the accusations they bring against one another, partly by the brokerage of places to individuals and favors to localities in which deputies act as intermediaries between Ministers and local wire-pullers, while scandals occurring from time to time have, although few deputies have been tarnished, lowered the respect felt for the Chamber as a whole.

The same kind of brokerage is rife in Italy also. The deputy holds his place by getting grants or other advantages for his district, and is always busy in influencing patronage by intrigue.

In Great Britain these last-named evils have not appeared, partly because the Civil Service was taken entirely out of politics many years ago, partly because the passing of "private bills" for local or personal purposes is surrounded by elaborate safeguards. Yet the House of Commons seems to hold a slightly lower place in the esteem of the people than it did in the days of Melbourne and Peel. Its intellectual quality has not risen. Its proceedings are less fully reported. The frequency of obstruction and of the use of the closure to overcome obstruction have reduced the value of the debates and affected the quality of legislation, while also lessening respect for a body which is thought—though this is inevitable under the party system—to waste time in unprofitable wrangling. The "sterile hubbub of politics" was noted by a nonpolitical critic even thirty years ago.[1] The independence of members has suffered by the more stringent party discipline. The results of these causes are seen in the diminished deference accorded to Parliament, perhaps also in its slightly diminished attractiveness for able and public-spirited men.

In the new overseas democracies—Canada, Australia, and New Zealand—we cannot, except perhaps in New Zealand, now talk of a falling off, for the level was never high. Corruption is rare, but the standard both of tone and manners and of intellectual attainment is not worthy of communities where everybody is well off and well educated, and where grave problems of legislaton call for constructive ability.

III

Setting aside the special conditions of each particular country, because in each the presence or absence of certain institutions may give rise to special defects, let us seek for some general causes which in all the countries named, though in some more than others, have been tending to reduce the prestige and authority of legislative bodies.

The spirit of democratic equality has made the masses of the people less deferential to the class whence legislators used to be drawn, and the legislatures themselves are today filled from all classes except the very poorest. This is in some respects a gain, for it enables popular wishes to be better expressed, but it makes a difference to Parliamentary habits. In England, for example, the old "country gentlemen," who used to form more than half the House of Commons and from whom many brilliant figures came, are now a small minority. Constituencies are everywhere larger than formerly, owing to the growth of population and to universal suffrage; while the personal qualities of a candidate do less to commend him to electors who are apt to vote at the bidding of party or because the candidate is lavish in his promises. Not only do the members of legislatures stand more than heretofore on the same intellectual level as their constituents, but their personal traits and habits and the way in which they do business are better known through the Press.

In some countries much of the space once allotted to the reports of debates is now given to familiar sketches, describing the appearance and personal traits of members, in which any eccentricity is "stressed." "Scenes" are made the most of, and the disorders which mark them have left a painful impression. Legislators, no longer conventionally supposed to dwell in an Olympian dignity, set little store by the standards of decorum that prevailed when, as in France and England two generations ago, a large proportion of the Chamber belonged to the same cultivated social circles, and recognized an etiquette which prescribed the maintenance of external forms of politeness. The defect perpetuates itself, because men are apt to live up to no higher standard than that which they find. The less the country respects them, the less they respect themselves. If politicians are assumed to move on a low plane, on it they will continue to move till some great events recall the country and them to the ideals which inspired their predecessors.

The disappearance of this sense of social responsibility has affected the conduct of business. Every rule of procedure, every technicality is now insisted upon and "worked for all it is worth." This stiffening or hardening of the modes of doing business has made parliamentary deliberations seem more and more of a game, and less and less a consultation by the leaders of the nation on matters of public welfare.

A like tendency is seen in the stricter party discipline enforced in the British self-governing Dominions. As party organizations are stronger, the discretion of representatives is narrowed: they must vote with their leaders. The member who speaks as he thinks is growing rare in English-speaking countries. Whips called him a self-seeker, or a crank, yet his criticisms had their value.

The payment of members has been supposed to lower the status and fetter the freedom of a representative. First introduced in the United States, where it was inevitable because in so large a country members had to leave their business and their often distant homes, to live in the national or in a State capital, it became inevitable in European countries also when the enfranchised wage-earners desired to send members of their own class into Parliament. How far it has affected the character of the representatives is not yet clear, but it everywhere exposes the poorer members to the imputation of an undue anxiety to retain their seats as a means of livelihood.

Just as the increased volume of platform speaking by leading politicians has lessened the importance of the part which Parliamentary debate used to play in forming public opinion, so has the growth of the newspaper press encroached on the province of the Parliamentary orator. Only the very strongest statesmen can command an audience over the whole country, such as that which a widely read newspaper addresses every day. The average legislator fears the newspaper, but the newspaper does not fear the legislator, and the citizen who perceives this draws his own conclusions.

Other organizations occupying themselves with public questions and influencing large sections of opinion have arisen to compete with legislatures for the attention of the nation. The Conventions or Conferences of the old and "regular" parties, both in England and in America, have no great importance; for, being practically directed by the party leaders, they add little or nothing to the programs whereto the party has been already committed. But the meetings of industrial sections and of the new class parties, such as the Trades Union Congress in England and the Congress of the Peasant party in Switzerland, the Socialist Congresses in France, and the Labour Union Congresses or assemblies representing the farmers or miners in the United States, the gatherings of farmers in Canada, and the still more powerful meetings of Labour organizations in Australia—all these are important, for they represent a large potential vote and their deliverances serve as a barometer showing the rise or fall of opinion on industrial issues. Those who lead them may win and wield a power equal to that of all but the most outstanding Parliamentary chiefs.

Whether or no it be true, as is commonly stated, that in European countries the intellectual level of legislative assemblies has been sinking, it is clear that nowhere does enough of that which is best in the character and talent of the nation find its way into those assemblies. In this respect the anticipations of eighty years ago have not been realized. The entrance to political life is easier now than it was then, but the daily round of work less agreeable, while the number of alternative careers is larger.

IV

These changes, taken all together, account for the disappointment felt by whoever compares the position held by legislatures now with the hopes once entertained of the services they were to render. Yet may we not ask whether there was ever solid ground for these hopes? Were they not largely due to the contrast which the earliest free assemblies offered to the arbitrary or obscurantist governments which had been ruling everywhere but in America, Britain, and Switzerland, and against which the noblest intellects in the oppressed countries were contending? It was natural to expect that when men of such a type came to fill the legislatures of France, Germany, Italy, and Spain, they would rival the assemblies of the countries that were already thriving on freedom. That expectation was largely fulfilled as regards the first free assemblies, for those who led them were exceptional men, produced or stimulated by the calls of their time. The next generation did not in days of peace rise to the standard set in the days of conflict.

The issues of policy which now occupy legislatures are more complex and difficult than those of half a century ago. The strife of classes and formation of class parties were not foreseen, nor the vast scale on which economic problems would present themselves, nor the constant additions to the functions of governments, nor that immense increase of wealth which has in some countries exposed legislators to temptations more severe than any that had assailed their predecessors. The work to be done then was largely a work of destruction. Old abuses had to be swept away, old shackles struck off, and for effecting this a few general principles were thought to suffice. The next generation was confronted by constructive work, a remodeling of old institutions in the effort to satisfy calls for social reorganization, a difficult task which needed more hard thinking and creative power than were forthcoming. Thus while the demands on representative assemblies were heavier the average standard of talent and character in their members did not rise. Never was it clearer than it is today that Nature shows no disposition to produce men with a greatness proportioned to the scale of the problems they have to solve.

Taking all these causes into account, whatever decline is visible in the quality and the influence of legislatures becomes explicable without the assumption that the character of free peoples has degenerated under democracy.

V

It remains to inquire what have been the results of the reduced authority of representative assemblies. The power which has departed from them must have gone elsewhere. Whither has it gone?

In the several States of the American Union it has gone to the Executive or to the People. The State Governor has become a leading figure whenever he happens to be a strong man with some initiative, some force of will, some gift for inspiring that confidence which legislatures fail to command. Not often perhaps does such a man appear, but when he appears he counts for more than he would have done forty years ago. In an increasing number of States, the introduction of the Initiative and Referendum has narrowed the power of the representatives and transferred legislation to the citizens voting at the polls, while the Recall has made members displaceable by a popular vote before their term comes to an end. All State legislatures have lost the function of choosing a United States Senator, which has been now assigned to the popular vote, this being the only considerable change made in the Federal system. Congress has fallen rather than risen, and the power of the President, when he knows how to use it, and happens to be a strong man who takes the fancy of the people, has been tending to grow.

The Constitutions of France and Great Britain have remained the same in form and on the whole in practice. But in France the recurring dissatisfaction with the frequent changes of Ministry which intrigues in the Chamber bring about continues to evoke cries for a more stable Executive. The discontent with "Parliamentarism" which nearly led to a coup d'état in 1888, may have serious consequences, especially if the steadying influence excited by the fear of external aggression should cease to operate.

In Britain the House of Commons is still the center of political life, and the driving-wheel of Government. But the power of the Cabinet over the majority has grown as parties have stiffened their discipline, for majorities are strong in proportion to their docility. If that so-called "control of the caucus" which British pessimists bewail really exists, it is not so much the tyranny of a party organization acting under the committees that manage it in the constituencies as an instrument in the hands of the party chiefs.

In Italy a somewhat different process seems to have made the Chamber more subservient than formerly to the Ministry, for although the party system holds no great power, deputies are brought into line by the manipulation of patronage and benefits bestowed on powerful business interests or on localities. The Spanish Cortes, divided into a number of groups, each following its leader, are little regarded by the people, who have shown (except in Catalonia) scant interest in the exercise of their now widely extended suffrage.

In these European cases it is rather the moral ascendancy than the legal power of the legislature that has been affected. But when moral power droops legal power ceases to inspire affection or respect.

VI

Can any useful conclusions, any lessons available for practice be drawn from these facts?

The mischiefs arising in the United States, and (to a less extent) in Canada from the abuse for electoral purposes of legislative power in local and personal matters might be removed by stringent regulations, such as those which the British Parliament has imposed on the examination and enactment of private Bills.

A scandal complained of in some countries might be reduced if a system of strict competitive examinations for posts in the Civil Service were to cut away the opportunities members have of misusing their position for the purposes of patronage, while the transfer to local self-governing bodies of the powers exercised in administrative areas by the central government, together with the discontinuance of grants from the national treasury for local purposes would, while saving public money, dry up a copious fountain of jobbery, for where the money to be spent comes from local taxes its expenditure is more likely to be carefully watched.[2] Anyhow the central legislature would be relieved from one form of temptation.

These are what may be called mechanical remedies for evils arising from defects in the mechanism of Parliamentary institutions. With those causes of decline which are either independent of the legislatures themselves, or arise from the intensity of party spirit, or the indisposition of men qualified to serve their country to offer themselves as candidates—for these causes the remedies have to be sought elsewhere. Representative Assemblies must remain the vital center of the frame of government in every country not small enough to permit of the constant action of direct popular legislation; and even in such countries they cannot be altogether dispensed with. The utility which Mill and Bagehot saw in them remains, if perhaps reduced. The people as a whole cannot attend to details, still less exercise over the Executive the watchful supervision needed to ensure honest and efficient administration.

NOTES

1. Matthew Arnold.
2. Where, however, the undertaking extends over a wide area and has a national importance, national subventions may be unavoidable.

2

Reform of the House of Commons: The Case for Specialization

JOHN P. MACKINTOSH

While Bryce concerned himself with the impact of modern democracy on parliament, J. P. Mackintosh considers the effect of the complexity of the issues facing contemporary legislatures. As a political scientist, the author of a major study (The British Cabinet), and a Member of Parliament since 1966, Mackintosh advocates specialization within the House of Commons to enable it to hold its own against the expertise available to the executive branch of government. He argues for a system of specialized committees to oversee the ministries and evaluate their legislative proposals. Mackintosh rejects the traditional constitutional arguments raised in Great Britain against powerful legislative committees, regarding these arguments merely as excuses for maintaining cabinet domination over parliament.

For most of those interested in reforming the House of Commons in the sense of redressing the balance between the increasing power of the executive and the growing impotence of

This chapter is a condensation of an "occasional paper" published in 1970 by the Edinburgh University Press. It is reprinted by permission of the author.

backbenchers, select committees sometimes called "specialist" committees have always been the most hopeful device. This is true historically, and it is interesting that when the House first decided to appoint two committees to aid in the process of legislation in 1883, they were intended to be specialist committees in that they each had specific subjects to deal with—Law and Trade—and were supposed to proceed by hearing witnesses and by investigating the content of the Bills submitted to them. When, however, the House actually appointed the Committees (for one session and regularly after 1888), these recommendations for the operations of the Committees were abandoned and in 1907 their specialist designations were removed, the titles being changed to letters of the alphabet.[1] However, in the following years, whenever it was felt that the House was definitely failing to discharge one of its major functions, the device of a committee was adopted. But a system of standing specialist committees failed to establish itself in the ensuing half century.

In the early 1960s, as a tendency to reexamine British institutions in a critical light developed, a series of books and articles once again pressed the case for select committees. In the debate on the Queen's Speech immediately after the general election of 1966, the Prime Minister said that the Government intended to establish "one or two new Parliamentary Committees to concern themselves with administration in the sphere of certain Departments whose usual operations are not only of national concern but in many cases are of intensely human concern."[2] On December 14, 1966, Mr. Crossman, who had been appointed Leader of the House of Commons, proposed the creation of two select (specialist) committees, one on Agriculture and one on Science and Technology.[3] Later on, select committees were created to watch over the Parliamentary Commissioner (the Ombudsman) and over the working of the Race Relations Act. In 1967 a further select committee was set up to scrutinize the work of the Ministry of Education. When the Agriculture Committee was closed down in early 1968, its place was taken by a committee on Scottish Affairs, while a committee on Overseas Aid was formed in April 1969 to take the place of the Committee on Education. The reformers had clearly achieved much, and there had been enough experience by 1970 to permit some interim judgment on whether the experiment has been a success.

THE CASE FOR AND AGAINST SPECIALIST COMMITTEES

Before examining the record of these committees, it is worth recalling the major reasons why they were so consistently advocated by reformers and why they were successfully resisted till 1966. Many diverse arguments were used to support the proposal but the main point was relatively simple. The House of Commons had steadily lost influence over the executive because of the increasing strength of the party system. In the nineteenth century, the House had dismissed Governments without having to face a general election, it had sacked individual ministers and had introduced and carried bills against the Government, and it had taken Government measures and defeated or rewritten them. The two main signs of this power were that the House controlled its own timetable and could force a Government to disclose full details of its policies even in such sensitive areas as foreign policy and defense.

All this was altered as the mass electorate voted more and more according to party labels and thus gave the party leaders, that is the Prime Minister and his colleagues, direct control over MPs. The Government used this control to force the House of Commons to surrender decisions about the timetable to the executive and to give up the House's power to appoint select committees and to order the publication of government papers. Gradually the Commons became reduced to registering the results of general elections and to passing virtually all the legislation put before it. Under these conditions, the Opposition uses the House to explain to the public its case against the Government, while ministers use it to put over their policies. The only influence remaining to the House occurs in special situations when Government backbenchers manage to convince the Cabinet that it is in the Government's own interest to modify some proposal and such cases of influence are hard to pin down because there are so many other pressures brought to bear on ministers.

Facing this situation, the reformers appreciated that it was not possible to go back to the more open and independent voting of the mid-nineteenth century. Nor was there much use producing more time for backbench contributions if the timetable itself was in the hands of the Government. Direct control over ministers could scarcely be restored to MPs since they had no secure base, no independent position in their constituencies which would enable them to resist party pressure.

But ministers are still influenced by public opinion and by the need to win general elections so that the House of Commons could be given a slightly larger place in the decision-making process if, without in any way tampering with party loyalties, it could find out and publicize the real choices open to the Government at any particular time. For instance, in the field of agricultural policy, if the House knew what options were being considered when farm prices were fixed each year, they could understand the alternatives and appreciate the various forces so that the public could learn what was happening and see what return it was getting for the money expended. In this way, the Commons could be given investigatory functions which would open up an issue allowing outside opinion to focus on the problem before a decision was taken and would inform MPs so that debates and questions in the House would be more relevant and therefore testing for Ministers. These powers would also force Departments and pressure groups to explain their assumptions, to carry out the necessary research and justify their decisions, and would bring public attention back to the Commons as the place where these investigations were made. If this happened, debates would be better informed and would attract more interest as the outside pressure groups and the public in general found that pressure through the House could occasionally persuade Governments to modify their policies.

To all those, mainly academics, who had thought about the problem, this seemed to be the only way forward. Moreover, the standard objections, coming mainly from politicians, appeared to be misguided or trivial. The first of these objections was the "we do not want to be like the French (pre-1958) or the Americans" response, which could be dismissed by the supporters of specialist committees as an unreal fear since the British political system was quite different from the French or the American and the effect of investigatory committees would therefore be quite different also. Then there was the suggestion that these committees would become involved in policy disputes, start making recommendations, and even try to steal executive authority from the Ministers. The obvious answer was that while the party system remained, no Minister need pay any attention if he did not want to. The existing committees (on Estimates and Nationalized Industries) realized this fully and therefore avoided making themselves look foolish by pronouncements on sensitive party issues. Finally there was the curious argument that the House as a whole would resent any attempt to derogate from its position as the ultimate arbiter on policy questions. This seemed the most flimsy objection since it is generally accepted that the House does not exist as a corporate body actually taking decisions on important matters apart from the Government. This is why it has not, in practice, resented encroachment by the existing investigatory committees. In any case, the real encroachment is coming from the stream of advisory bodies and commissions being set up by successive Governments just because the House is not in a position to investigate problems and produce informed recommendations.

The reason why these threadbare contentions carried the day till 1966 is that they were not the real explanation for the opposition. It is not always appreciated that politicians groping for a counterargument often reach back for out-of-date constitutional maxims which seem to cover their position (as when a Minister not wanting to disclose something in a recess says it is his duty to make his first report to the House of Commons).

The real reasons underlying the opposition to select commit-

tees are powerful and come from several quarters in the House
of Commons and from Whitehall. In the first place, it is mainly
outsiders interested in the democratic process who consider that
the Commons' primary function is to act as a check on Governments between elections and who therefore assume that this is
one of the main objectives of MPs. In fact the vast majority of
MPs do not accept this. Ministers, shadow ministers, and the
throng of would-be ministers on each side regard the House as a
place where the Government defends its position and the Opposition, far from any desire to alter existing policies, wants to
make its case to assume in full the same set of governmental
powers after the next election. And for the remainder, the bulk
of MPs who do not expect to go any further up the political lad-
der, they likewise have little desire to alter existing policies. On
both sides, they are loyal supporters of their front benches and
they see the Commons as an extension of the struggle for power
which takes place at elections. For all these groups, the idea of
select committees of the specialist investigatory kind seems a foreign intrusion into the set-piece confrontations which, for them,
are the life of politics.

Moreover, in a sense, they are right in that it is disingenuous
of the reformers to keep saying (as most of them have done)
that they had no intention of altering the relations between the
executive and the House of Commons. If this was true, there
would be no point in making the proposals. In fact, it is not possible to make any changes in the procedure or facilities of
the House without, in some slight degree, affecting this
relationship.[4] It is true that a range of select committees would
not expose the Government to defeat in the lobbies but there
would be an extra source of pressure on ministers. Instead of
fixing up legislative proposals in cozy conclaves with the pressure
groups and then coming to the House with a "take-it-or-leave-it"
approach, there would have to be public explanations and discussions at a formative stage in policy-making. To introduce
such extra and less predictable considerations would mean more
work and the strain of increased uncertainty. Civil servants would

have to learn the new technique of public exposition before rank and file MPs on committees and ministers would have to be able to face much more searching cross-examination than can ever take place under the rules of Question Time. So the critics were right to argue that this was something new in British politics and this is why they turned to what the academics rightly dismiss as misleading foreign comparisons or appeals to outdated maxims about the authority of the House as a whole.

In addition, many MPs have other more personal reasons for reacting against these reform proposals. For the ambitious back-bencher, the task is to impress ministers and particularly the Prime Minister. For this purpose service on select committees is of no use unless the MP becomes a thorn in the Government's flesh and then the impression created is detrimental. Moreover, most MPs, ambitious or not, are very jealous lest any colleague should steal a march on them. Clearly no Member can serve on more than one or two committees and it would be most galling for some backbenchers to feel that they were being outshone in debates or simply not being called by Mr. Speaker because other MPs either knew more or had a prior claim to speak by virtue of service on the appropriate select committee. In general, MPs are political animals and far more interested in scoring political points than in understanding the administrative processes and narrow options open to any Government. Ministers, for their part, find it easier to dismiss broad political attacks than to rebut a careful dissection of their precise choices. Many of the orators in the House prefer such broad, if fruitless, attacks to detailed attempts to influence or alter governmental decisions.[5] Politics in part depends on the capacity to sharpen up differences, to paint pictures that are almost caricatures, while government is often the laborious process of explaining how little movement is possible. An understandable fear is that MPs on committees will get so involved in comprehending the latter that they become incapable of the former.

It is important, therefore, to appreciate that select committees of the kind under discussion were not appointed in December

1966 because the House of Commons overwhelmingly wanted them or forced them on the Government. Probably only some sixty to eighty Labour members, mostly new members first elected in 1964 or 1966, were definitely in favor with a far smaller number of Conservatives in support. The committees were introduced because the Prime Minister felt they were part of the the reforming image the Labour Party was trying to acquire in those years, because he thought they would keep some of the more restless among the new Members happy, and because both the Leader of the House and the Chief Whip were (by December, 1966) committed Parliamentary reformers.[6] But there were still many opponents in the Cabinet and on the backbenches. The policy was not part of a definite, coherent, new attitude in the party or among the leadership but was very tentative.

After a period of operation of these committees, it is now possible to examine their history and see whether they have fulfilled the reformers' hopes, justified their opponents' fears, or whether the results have developed in any unexpected fashion.

THE COMMITTEE ON SCIENCE AND TECHNOLOGY

One of the first two committees to be appointed was asked "to consider Science and Technology and to report thereon." The choice of this subject was largely because a joint parliamentary and outside committee called the "Parliamentary and Scientific Committee" had strongly recommended such a move.[7] The fourteen members were nominated in January 1967 and as this was for only one session, they chose a subject "of prime national importance," which "involved large sums of public money," where changes in public policy might well be needed and yet there was a chance of reporting by the autumn of that year. The topic selected was the development of nuclear reactors with all the side issues involved.

There were several procedural problems during the following eight months.[8] The Committee decided to send two subcommittees to look at nuclear reactor programs, one to Europe and one to the United States. On May 4, 1967, the motions requesting permission to travel were handed to the Chief Whip and the Foreign Office was asked for its help. For two months the Government Whips refused to table the motion and only after strenuous protests to the Leader of the House was this obstacle overcome. Even then, the Foreign Office refused to accept the decision till further pressure had been applied. The visits did produce valuable information and in retrospect the fears entertained by the Foreign Office were seen to be groundless.[9]

Second, under the power awarded to select committees by the House of Commons "to send for persons, papers, and records," the committee had asked for a document from the Minister of Power. After six months "he submitted a paper . . . which was very nearly an insult to the Committee, because it was so slender,"[10] he failed to mention another paper already prepared by his Ministry, and he refused to produce a document which Lord Robens had mentioned in his evidence. This latter was a background paper for a conference between the nationalized industries on fuel costs and it was repeatedly asked for by the Clerk to the Committee. Finally the Chairman wrote a three-line letter demanding the document, a letter which was copied and circulated by the Minister of Power (Mr. Marsh) to the Cabinet to illustrate the shocking behavior of select committees. It was ultimately produced too late to be of any use to the Committee in its deliberations and the members were so irritated that they ignored the classification "confidential" and published the paper as an appendix to their Report.

The only other complaint of the Committee was that it had hurried in order to produce a Report by October 1967 which was not debated in the House till the following May and then only after a debate had been held in the House of Lords.[11] The Report itself was a massive document, the product of 33 sittings lasting a total of 70 hours; it covered not only the development of nuclear reactors for electricity supply and the U.K. programs for constructing nuclear powered generating stations but the organization and structure of the industry, its relations with government departments, the types of reactors that should be produced, the problems in mounting a program and in exporting reactors, and finally it considered the place of nuclear energy in the national fuel policy.[12] On the institutional side, the Committee felt that neither the Ministry of Power nor the Ministry of Technology were adequately equipped to monitor the work of the Atomic Energy Authority and therefore suggested a technical assessment unit to study the merits of A.E.A. projects and a specialist Parliamentary Committee similar to the American Joint Committee on Atomic Energy to scrutinize all energy problems and explain them to the House.

In the debate on the Report in May 1968[13] few attended, ten of the fourteen speakers being committee members. There was general criticism of the seven-month delay in holding the debate particularly since the Minister of Technology (Mr. Wedgwood Benn) had said he was waiting in order to announce his decisions but no such announcements were in fact made. There had been one party division in the Committee over the future structure of the industry but the Chairman argued that this was not due to any whipping but to a genuine division between those who believed in a market solution and those who believed in a managed solution. It was evident from the speeches that there had been a great deal of unanimity and all members were agreed on the value of the exercise. Mr. Wedgwood Benn, speaking for the Government, rejected the institutional recommendations but said that "the power of Parliament relative to the Executive has been effectively restored in that . . . hon. Members are at least as well briefed as the Minister."[14]

Having finished nuclear reactors, the full Committee had to begin a second major piece of work and to devise a method of finding suitable subjects and of maintaining some continuity. As its next subject, the Committee decided to examine defense research establishments, particularly considering the use of scientific manpower and other resources. To maintain continuity, a general purposes subcommittee was set up with three tasks. One was to chase up previous recommendations of the full Committee and see what action had been taken. The second was to make preliminary inquiries into problems to see whether they merited full-scale examination. The third was to act as a kind of steering committee advising the Chairman. This subcommittee in mid-1968 looked at three topics of contemporary interest: the development of carbon fibers, the work on fusion research at Culham laboratory, and the decision of the Government to withdraw from the 300 G.C.V. acceleration project.[15] At the same time, as part of the main defense research project, two subcommittees were sent on fact-finding visits to Europe and the U.S.A., on this occasion without any resistance from the Foreign Office and with the positive aid of the Ministry of Defence.

By the end of 1969 it was clear that this Committee had become a permanent feature of the House of Commons like the Select Committee on Nationalized Industries. While other specialist committees (as will be explained below) were given a limited period of life, the Select Committee on Science and Technology was put in a separate category as a "subject" rather than a "departmental" committee. Though it had had its brushes with the Foreign Office (over visits abroad), with the Ministry of Power (over papers), and with the Treasury (over staffing), it ranged across several ministries and was positively welcomed by the Ministry of Technology. Thus, while there were opponents and some who were irritated by its criticisms, the Committee had established itself as a serious, well-informed, and hard-working body. All the members (who attended regularly) felt that it was worthwhile and that parliamentary scrutiny of executive actions had been both extended and deepened.

THE COMMITTEE ON AGRICULTURE

The Select Committee on Agriculture which was set up at the same time in December 1966, had a less happy history. It was different, being "departmental." Its terms of reference were "to consider the activities in England and Wales of the Ministry of

Agriculture, Fisheries, and Food and to report thereon this session." The reason for choosing the Department of Agriculture was that the Prime Minister had insisted that the minister in charge of the particular department should agree to be the guinea pig and Mr. Fred Peart, the Minister for Agriculture, had long been a supporter of select committees.

There were rumors that the Minister of Agriculture and the Leader of the House (Mr. Crossman) would have preferred the Committee to undertake a fact-finding exercise on a special topic such as the control of epidemic disease among livestock. However, after some acrimonious discussion, the members insisted on grappling with the hottest contemporary issue, the effects on British agriculture of entry to the Common Market, a form of words being found to bring it within the terms of reference. Although the Committee was divided not so much on party lines as between those for and those against joining the Common Market, this cleavage disappeared as the work of discovering the precise effects progressed. While some members were able to capture headlines such as "milk rationing if Britain joins E.E.C.," all appreciated that for the Committee to pronounce for or against entry would simply make it look ridiculous.[16] The task was to put the facts before Parliament and the public.

The investigation was, as in the case of the first report from the Committee on Science and Technology, rushed in order to be within the sessional deadline imposed by the Government. The Committee in its Report[17] mentioned the tight limit of five months time and the shortage of staff. It then went on to explain two particular difficulties encountered in dealings with Whitehall.

The first was over papers. The Committee heard from Sir James Marjoribanks, the head of the Brussels delegation, that his agricultural staff was not sufficient and that he had asked for an extra attaché. The Ministry of Agriculture, which appeared to give a much lower priority to the question of E.E.C. membership, had replied refusing his request. On April 26, 1967, the Committee asked to see the correspondence. The Foreign Secretary, after several reminders, refused on June 26 to submit the papers and repeated his refusal on July 26. The Committee had offered to treat the information as confidential or to have the names of any individuals "blanked out," but none of these proposals made any difference and the dispute was never resolved.

The second difficulty also involved the Foreign Office.[18] The members of the Committee decided that they wanted to see whether the Ministry's account of the Common Agricultural Policy of the European Economic Community accorded with the Community's own account. The Foreign Office was told of the intention to visit Brussels and the Committee wrote to the E.E.C. Commission on March 22, 1967, explaining its purpose and asking if a visit would be possible. Apparently the E.E.C. Commission then checked with the Foreign Office as nothing more was heard by the Committee until May when the Foreign Office indicated that such a visit might be misconstrued by unfriendly governments in Europe as an attempt to open negotiations about British entry to the Market. In conversations with successive Ministers of State, Lord Chalfont and Mr. Mulley, the Committee explained their objectives, said they wished to avoid any misunderstanding, and offered to go formally to call on the British delegation, fact-finding contacts with the E.E.C. Commission being kept on an informal basis. Yet on June 21, the Foreign Office still objected and said it would refuse to allow the visit. A further meeting was held with the Leader of the House and a compromise was reached that a small subcommittee would go. But the Government offered no help (as they usually do) over moving the necessary motion in the House, the Chairman of the Committee having to remain up all night to move the motion at 6:15 A.M. on Tuesday, July 11, less than four hours before the members of the Committee were due to leave for Brussels. Even then further difficulties had to be resolved at the airport and in Brussels,[19] though the visit was both useful to the members and caused no embarrassment, showing that the Foreign Office's fears were entirely groundless.

Having dealt with these problems, the Report then turned to the preparations made by the Ministry in the light of Britain's possible entry to the E.E.C. These were found to be thorough, the major calculations being "based on solid foundations." But the Report detected a lack of appreciation of the flexibility of the Common Agricultural Policy on the part of the Ministry. It also observed that there were too few agricultural specialists in Brussels and in E.E.C. capitals, too few visits by British officials, and too little preparatory consultation between the Ministry and interested bodies in the United Kingdom. The Report then concluded with a detailed review of the evidence and of the probable impact on British farming, commodity by commodity.

Although the Report had not been seriously critical of the Ministry of Agriculture and though there had been no overt clashes with its officials, members of the Committee had felt some tension. They had consistently tried to get behind the uniform front presented by witnesses and to find out what discussions and disagreements had taken place in the Ministry itself. When these probes were parried, the Committee's reaction was usually to press for more memoranda, over thirty documents being supplied during the five months, all of which imposed a considerable burden on the Ministry. It was also clear that the Foreign Office and the Leader of the House of Commons (Mr. Crossman) had been considerably irritated by the Committee's persistence over the visit to Brussels. As a result, members of the Committee were not surprised that there were stories in the press during the 1967 summer recess that the Committee would not be reappointed in the new session.

A debate was held (for a half day) on the Report on May 14, 1968, ten months after it had been laid on the table of the House. The Minister (by then Mr. Cledwyn Hughes) moved to take note of the Report and stressed the "substantial additional burden" that the Committee had imposed on his officials.[20] Otherwise he simply stated that the "experiment (of having a Select Committee on Agriculture) has been proved to be a success." The Opposition spokesman, Mr. Godber, agreed, but asked about the future of the Committee, which clearly wished to go on and study several further subjects listed in their Report. In a debate on procedure on November 14, 1967, Mr. Crossman had suggested that the Committee had spent so much time quarreling with the Foreign Office that it "did not manage to cover more than a tiny fraction of the Ministry's activities, and we have therefore proposed that it should spend a second year studying the Ministry of Agriculture before moving to other fields of investigation."[21] But the Government made no indication of its intentions for the long-run future of the Committee.

During the 1967–1968 session, the problem of expanding agricultural production and of replacing imports was examined. Two subcommittees on fisheries and horticulture were appointed and they reported in July and October 1968, but the full Committee concluded "that they cannot adequately consider . . . the N.E.D.C. Report on the same subject (which had just been published) . . . and related topics before the end of the present session of Parliament. They, therefore, ask that they should be reappointed in the next session to continue their work."[22] Meanwhile, the Fisheries subcommittee recommended that more attention should be paid to the industry; that there should be a statutory minimum prices scheme, better control of quality, an examination of possible quotas, levies, and minimum import prices; that consideration be given to either abolishing the White Fish Authority or giving it more power; and that a Minister of State for Fisheries be appointed. It might have been possible for the Committee to have reported on its major inquiry at the same time, but the members felt that they had been unduly hurried in the previous session and that there was more evidence to be heard. There was also the tactical point that if the Government was toying with the idea of not reappointing the Committee, such an action would be much harder to defend if the Committee was in the middle of an important study.

These fears proved to be justified. The new session began on October 30, 1968. On November 6, the Chairman was told that the Committee would be reappointed but given only till December 31 to report, when it would be finally abolished. The rest of the Committee first heard of this when the motion appeared on the Order Paper for November 7. On the first occasion members of the Committee "talked the order out" and thereafter opposed the motion every night for a week. Any objections to "unopposed business" coming after 10 P.M. mean that the motion has to stand over till the next day. The Government can force through such a motion before 10 P.M. but if this is done there must be some time for a debate. Members continued to object and put down an amendment, the Government ultimately deciding (again without consultation) to extend the time limit to February 28, and in this form the motion was slipped through at the end of business on a Friday when most members had returned to their constituencies.

In February 1969 the Committee made two reports, one dealing with the agricultural issues it had been examining[23] and the other with the procedural difficulties it had encountered.[24]

The latter Report made six recommendations "for the more efficient working of the Specialist Committee system":

I. That Specialist Committees should have a measure of permanence. The practice whereby Departmental Specialist Committees cease to exist after a session or two is destructive of the purpose of gaining a body of expertise, and the consequent uncertainty inhibits any rational planning of work.

II. That Specialist Committees should be consulted over changes in their duration, size, and membership.

III. That Specialist Committees should in general be subject Committees covering a topic rather than the work of a particular Department.

IV. That Specialist Committees should be limited in size to about 16 members.

V. That it is essential that a staff adequate to service Specialist Committees should be provided and that staff economies should not be allowed to limit the development of the new system.

VI. That Specialist Committees should not be inhibited by a Government from considering policy in its formative stages nor should they be prevented from considering matters due for legislation.

and concluded with the bitter remark that

> We deplore the decision to disband the Committee on Agriculture at a time when it was becoming familiar with its task, developing its expertise, and had identified so many questions which urgently call for further investigation.

The disbandment of the Committee created some ill-feeling between the Government and the more enthusiastic members who had attended regularly and had come to value the work. The effect had been to give those members whose primary interest was agriculture an opportunity to collect information and become, if not as well informed as ministers, at least confident of their facts and up-to-date. Agricultural questions were noticeably more apt during these two sessions and agricultural debates were of a higher quality. The MPs concerned also found that being members added a little to their standing in their constituencies, and for all these reasons, they resented the Government's decision. Indeed, there was some talk of trying to keep an unofficial committee going, but the problem of finding funds to pay a clerk and the difficulty of summoning witnesses made it impossible.

OTHER SPECIALIST COMMITTEES

The action taken over the Agriculture Committee affected the treatment of the whole select committee experiment. For instance, at a time when the Government was still contemplating the expansion of the select committee system, a Committee was appointed (in February 1968) to consider the activities of the Department of Education and Science and the Scottish Education Department. At first this Committee encountered only what could by then be described as the "usual difficulties." In its Third Special Report in July 1968,[25] it observed that it had been appointed four months after the start of the session and told to report before the end of that session. The results of this limitation were to reduce the possible subjects of inquiry, to make it difficult to obtain memoranda and arrange for witnesses to appear, and to make the Committee hurry with its report. In a Special Report they asked that, in future, the Committee should be set up earlier in the Session.

The Committee was indeed reappointed in the next session but not before some doubts had been raised. Mr. Trevor Park, one of the members, in the minute of time that was available between the motion being moved and 10 P.M., sought clarification of the Government's attitude to the future of the Committee in view of the fact that it was again being asked to report during the current session. The Deputy Chief Whip had replied that the motion was in "standard phraseology for the setting up of Committees of this kind" (though in fact this had not applied to Agriculture in its first two sessions). The Leader of the House, Mr. Fred Peart, then wrote to the Chairman to amplify the answer:

> I think perhaps I owe you a word of explanation as to why, in setting-up again the Select Committee on Education and Science —which I am glad to see has got under way without difficulty— we did so without your suggested change from a Departmental Committee to a subject Committee.
>
> The view we took on this is that subject Committees, e.g., Science and Technology, are long-standing, whereas Departmental Committees, which originally started out on an experimental basis of one Session, operate on the understanding that they will be appointed for no more than two Sessions. It is to avoid misunderstanding on this consequence that Education and Science has been left as a Departmental Committee.

This so surprised the Committee that they called Mr. Peart to give evidence on the point a few days later. The Chairman, Mr. Willey, said that "we have never appreciated the distinction between the two kinds of Committee" and "we are not aware of this understanding that a Departmental Committee would only last for two years." Mr. Peart replied that "I am all for Committees examining Departments but I always accepted . . . that they were experimental. . . . It was always intended that the Departmental Committees should be of limited duration . . .

and I would have thought that from the point of view of time two sessions is reasonable. . . . If a Committee we set up to be temporary were to become permanent I think it would frustrate the development of this experiment, and, indeed, prevent our setting up further Committees."

Pressed by members, the Leader of the House said that "it would be very wrong for two Departments only to be examined by Committees of this kind," showing that he did not envisage the possibility of more than two such Committees at any one time. He also said that as Agriculture was due to be closed, he would soon be announcing a new Committee. Mr. Park put it to the Minister that the distinction between "subject committees" and "departmental" committees was entirely artificial and had come into existence only after the first Committees had been appointed. Mr. Price asked what had been meant by "experimental" and what would be the criteria of success. "What makes it seem such a crying shame [is] that just as one feels that one has got the sort of expertise which is to be found in an American Congressional Committee, at that point one closes down and moves on to another Ministry. . . . This is all the time loading the scales in favor of an experienced Government Department as against an inexperienced Committee." Mr. Park observed that "you are going to close Committees at the very stage when they are becoming most effective."

To all this, the Leader of the House simply replied that the whole system was experimental and he took refuge in the old maxim that "in the end it must be Parliament who decides." The Chairman countered by pointing out that in fact a Select Committee's "continued existence depends upon the Government." Having published this evidence, the Committee in its Third Special Report said that all these limitations came as a surprise and were to be regretted and they urged "the Government to give careful consideration to methods whereby the House itself may be enabled to decide which specialist Committees it wants and which type they should be."[26]

The Committee which was announced in early 1969 to take

the place of the Agriculture Committee was one on Scottish Affairs and later it was indicated that once the Committee on Education and Science had finished its work, it would be replaced by a departmental committee to look at the Ministry of Overseas Development.[27] In each case it was made clear that these new committees would last till the end of the Parliament, by then not more than two years off.

Thus, by the end of the final session of the Parliament of 1966–70 there were still the Select Committee on Science and Technology and two departmental Select Committees, but the experimental nature of these bodies had been emphasized and their standing downgraded. This had happened not just because of the ruling that the latter category could last for only two sessions but also because Committees on such major areas of administration as Agriculture and Education had been replaced by a Committee on Scottish Affairs, whose origins had been largely political expediency, and a Committee on the Ministry of Overseas Development, which, however important it should be, is in practice one of the minor Whitehall Departments.

Two further categories of Select Committees existed. The first consisted of two new committees appointed to watch over the development of specific institutional practices, one to examine the reports laid before the House by the Parliamentary Commissioner for Administration (the Ombudsman) and another to watch over the operation of the Race Relations Act. Both these Committees took a rather broad view of their terms of reference. Both helped to press home the Act they had to supervise. Their capacity to review actions by departments or, in the case of Race Relations, the impact of the Act on specific problem areas, and their capacity to recommend extensions of the scope of operation gave and added strength and impetus to what Parliament had done.

The secondary category consisted of the three established committees on Estimates, Public Accounts, and Nationalized Industries which are not new and will not be examined further here.

CAN SPECIALIST COMMITTEES EXIST
IN THE BRITISH SYSTEM?

This, then, is the recent history of Select Committees. Has the experience proved anything and have the new committees lived up to the expectations of the reformers or has the whole experiment been a failure? Mr. Henry Fairlie is quite clear in his views:

> The attempt to create important committees. . . is an attempt to fashion mock political institutions within a constitution which cannot tolerate real ones. We would cease to waste a considerable amount of time if we admitted that such institutions—the roles they are meant to fill, and the functions they are meant to perform—can be given no significant existence within a political system which is controlled by a powerful democracy.[28]

There is something superficially convincing in this view. It does seem ridiculous to try to set up bodies to curb the executive which owe their very existence to the executive. The Government decides what committees it will have, it dispenses with some as soon as they are becoming effective (as happened to the Agriculture Committee), it sets up others which no one wants (Scottish Affairs), it chooses the chairmen, and it nominates the majority of the members, while the power to send for persons and papers means exactly what the Government or the Department in question chooses it to mean. Almost every chairman or committee member would far prefer a post in the Government to his position on a committee, and even if, at the end of all this, there is criticism of the Government, it can be ignored or set aside by the use of the ministerial majority.

This same analysis can explain the fate of the committees established before 1966. The old Public Accounts Committee was not devised by the House of Commons, it was thought up by Mr. Gladstone to help the Treasury discipline the other Departments and this it has continued to do. Likewise, the Estimates Committee was supposed to aid governmental drives for efficiency, but it was always prevented from specializing (except for two years, 1965–67) and becoming an effective check on the Government. After much tribulation, the Nationalized Industries Committee was allowed to start and then to continue because it assisted the Government in keeping these industries up to scratch. As soon as it wanted to investigate something the Government wished to keep to itself, the Bank of England, there was an adamant refusal, later moderated a little, provided no policy matters were considered.

On the whole, Governments do not mind committees of the House looking at totally new projects or coming up with useful ideas (to be used or forgotten as the executive desires), which is why the Select Committee on Science and Technology, despite its quarrels with the Foreign Office and with Mr. Marsh, was allowed to continue. But Committees which show a tenacious desire to find out about current policy formation and which want to discover who makes policy, to unearth the arguments, and to examine the efficiency of current administration, incur the immediate wrath of ministers and civil servants and are cashiered. After all, as Mr. Fairlie would conclude, politics is about power. In Britain power lies with the executive, apart from a quinquennial kickback by the mass electorate. The House of Commons has no independent source of power, and why should any Government in its right mind concede authority to a body that cannot exact it —why should ministers make rods for their own backs? Moreover, as has been argued, this view is held not only by the Government front bench but by Opposition leaders and by many on the backbenches also.

This argument is supplemented by Fairlie, by some backbenchers, and by *The Times*[29] with the point that if the House of Commons is to exercise any influence over ministers, it must be by the time-honored method of open political opposition on the floor of the House and in the lobbies. Although no majority Government has been defeated on the floor of the House (other than on some trivial point or on a snap vote) in this century, it is possible to point to occasional measures that have been modified or withdrawn because of such pressure. By far the most spectacular examples since 1945 occurred in 1969 when the Government first abandoned its House of Lords Reform Bill, not because of defeat but because it was taking too long, and then abandoned its Industrial Relations Bill because a majority of the Cabinet either turned against the measure or felt that it could not be forced through the House. If these do represent backbench victories and if they could be repeated reasonably regularly, perhaps they point toward a better way of readjusting the balance between the executive and the legislature than the development of a system of scrutinizing committees.[30]

The weakness in Mr. Fairlie's first line of argument is the assumption that the sole objective of politicians is to seize the maximum possible power. If this were the case, a British Government could use its majority to deprive the Opposition of their Supply Day—now simply Opposition Day—debates, whereas these opportunities for criticism have been extended from 26 to 29 days a session. If this were true, all sorts of methods present themselves for the extension of government power, and if they are not taken, it is because they are regarded as illegitimate, outside the bounds of political practice as it is currently understood in Britain. But the limits or content of proper political practice are continually altering, and to say that select committees with the power to scrutinize sections of the administration will never be acceptable is really simply a recommendation that they should not be accepted as part of the British system.

Thus the argument is not whether select committees are somehow alien elements which are bound to be spewed out of the present system. It is whether these committees are desirable additions to the existing complex of institutions and whether those responsible for setting the tone in British politics, for deciding what is or is not part of the system, are coming to accept these committees or are tending to regard them as undesirable.

SUPPORT FOR SPECIALIST COMMITTEES

The best way of answering these questions is to consider the currents of opinion in the House, in the Government, and in Whitehall and to assess what have been the lessons of the first committees. At the start, in December 1966, Mr. Crossman, then the Leader of the House, regarded specialist committees as "the most important aspect of parliamentary reform."[31] He asked the question, "should we experiment in giving to the backbench Member a share in the investigation of administration and even of the policies of the Government? I am convinced that this is a debt we must pay."[32]

But it was evident that at this stage the House took a cautious view, and apart from the views of backbenchers who had been associated with existing committees, most of the enthusiasm came from newer members elected in 1964 and 1966. On the Labour side, a backbench Parliamentary reform group was started under the chairmanship of Mr. William Hamilton to press for a steady progress. Four months later, at a meeting of this Group, the Leader of the House said he would like to add two more committees each session till every major department was covered by a scrutinizing committee, the last and toughest two to be set up (in terms of the opposition that would have to be overcome) being those dealing with defense and foreign affairs. Mr. Crossman invited the Reform Group to suggest the next two departments or areas to be covered, and after some discussion it was proposed that housing, trade, and industry were most suitable and interesting for Members.

Between this somewhat hopeful state of affairs and the start of the 1967–68 session, the atmosphere changed. By the autumn of 1967 two more committees were out of the question. Science and Technology had managed to become accepted as being "nondepartmental," but Agriculture with difficulty obtained a reprieve for only one more session. By November 1967, it was clear that the Government did not want to have more than two departmental committees in operation at any one time during the rest of the life of that Parliament. It is impossible to be specific as to precisely when or why this change took place, though the forces (and some of the people) on each side can be isolated.

On the side of carrying on with the experiment was the general progressive reforming tide of feeling which had helped the Labour Party to victory in 1964 and 1966. Moreover, once backbenchers had served on such committees, they became enthusiastic converts almost without exception. Few outside Westminister realize the extent to which MPs live in an artificial world cut off from outside information, experience, and contacts. Ministers can move about the country and information pours in through the department, through delegations, and is gathered on official visits. On the other hand, backbenchers are tied to the House during the week and to their constituencies on weekends. Gradually they lose touch with their previous occupations and professions. Harried with engagements and correspondence that add nothing to their knowledge, they gradually use up the stock of information they had on election and have little to put in its place. One great virtue of select committees is that they bring experts, pressure groups, and senior civil servants in a stream to the House to explain matters to Members. Members on the Committees found that at last they had their own sources of information. Far from this work detracting, as some left-wingers feared, from debates on the floor of the House, agriculture, education, industrial, and scientific debates all benefited enormously from the fact, as Mr. Wedgwood Benn put it,[33] that MPs were almost as well briefed as ministers. Question time also improved and Members found that in their constituencies their increasing expertise was acknowledged and appreciated. So the committee members themselves became the strongest supporters of the system. Men such as Ian Mikardo, the left-wing Chairman of the Select Committee on Nationalized Industries, showed no signs of changing into consensus politicians and members of the Education Committee confessed that the meetings were the highlight of their parliamentary week and gave them fresh interest in their work as MPs.[34]

OPPOSITION TO SPECIALIST COMMITTEES

The opponents of the system came from several sources. Some Cabinet ministers, such as Mr. Michael Stewart and Mr. Richard Marsh, felt that Parliament was a power struggle and these committees became, in effect, engines for criticizing the Government, thus simply aiding the Opposition. They believed that the task of the majority was simply to support their front bench. Some of the supporters of the system had, perhaps, failed to think out its full implications. Even Mr. Crossman at times talked as if the Committees' task was to go off and think up new ideas or document projects which might be of use to the executive rather than to press a particular department, week in and week out, about its conduct of affairs.

In this respect, some senior civil servants certainly found the committees hard to take. The departmental committees wanted to discover whether different sections of Whitehall had different views or different priorities. They wanted to know what arguments had gone on prior to decisions being taken. One method of getting at this information was to ask whether adequate thinking had been done before new policies were undertaken. All these questions and indeed the whole approach flew in the face of deeply ingrained civil service practice, senior officials having been trained to give the impression that Whitehall was entirely united on every ministerial policy and that all prior research and consultation had pointed to the identical conclusion. Nothing was more exasperating for committee members than to know privately that a terrible battle had taken place in a ministry or between a ministry and the Treasury only to find that not a hint of this or of the issues involved would be admitted in evidence before the Committee. Moreover, the objective of the MPs was not to get ammunition with which to attack the minister, but to find out the arguments and the extent to which alternative policies had been considered.

Finally, among the adverse forces, the Whips Office, though headed by a reformer, Mr. John Silkin, began to have its doubts. The problem that worried them, they said, was the manning of committees. By this, they did not mean the select committees, which were always oversubscribed, but the fact that MPs used service on these committees as an excuse for not attending the less interesting (for Government supporters) standing legislative committees.

THE FUTURE OF SPECIALIST COMMITTEES

Though there was little outside interest in specialist committees, within the House, on the other hand, the notion that they were really useful spread among backbenchers. In March 1969, the Labour Party Parliamentary Reform Group circularized all government backbenchers, asking for their views. (One hundred thirty-one members completed the questionnaire, 51 percent of the possible total.) Of those replying, 128 said the committees were carrying out an important parliamentary task, and only 3 disagreed. One hundred twenty-four said they would like to serve on a committee dealing with the subjects that interested them; 6 said no. Comparing standing legislative committees with select committees, 9 preferred service on the former, 100 on the latter.

During the same session the Select Committee on Procedure was examining the Commons' capacity to control public expenditure and was seeking to devise a new "circle of control" adapted to the five-year public expenditure program of the Treasury. Its Report proposed that the Government should publish an annual White Paper setting out the public expenditure program over a five-year period and that a medium term economic assessment showing what resources are available over the same period should also be published.[35] The Committee realized that the various proposals for expenditure listed in a functional form would require scrutiny and elucidation and it seemed quite appropriate, for Conservative as well as Labour members, to turn to the technique of select committee investigation for this purpose. They recommended a renovated Estimates Committee to be called a Select Committee on Expenditure. This was to have a General Subcommittee to watch over functional Subcommittees and to consider the form of the White Papers being put before the House, their arrangement, assumptions, and use of statistics. There were to be eight functional Subcommittees (all the Chairmen being on the General Subcommittee) each having nine members and each with an area of expenditure to examine.

Thus, at the end of the 1966–1970 Parliament, the Government was left with the choice of giving up the experiment of specialist committees altogether, of retaining some or a complete coverage of select (or "specialist") committees, of combining these with an expanded Select Committee on Expenditure, or of producing the new Expenditure Committee as an alternative to departmental and subject select committees.

Whatever solution develops under the Conservative Government in the early 1970s, the idea that there should be progress along these lines has taken a firm hold in the House. This is where Mr. Fairlie's argument that the executive will never voluntarily curtail its own power is oversimplified. If it becomes accepted by the vast majority of those in Parliament and in the political circles that increased scrutiny helps to preserve an efficient administration, that it gives an able minister a chance to explain his policies, and that the balance between executive and legislature requires this element, then the select committee experiment will be retained in some form or other. After the experience of the 1966–1970 Parliament, it is hard to imagine that such active and useful bodies will be completely swept aside. Even if all that emerges is a much larger, stronger Select Committee on Expenditure which can call for persons and papers, which specializes in particular sections of the administration, which can meet in public, which is properly staffed, and which can move from expenditure into any aspect of policy, this will be a great step in the direction desired by the reformers of the early 1960s.

Rebellion by Government backbenchers, which has always been possible at moments of crisis, is in no way a substitute for, nor does it conflict with, the need for a permanent increase in the Commons' capacity to find out what the executive is doing, to inform the public, and to bring pressure to bear at a wide variety of points. The traditionalists are wrong to suggest that Select Committees are in practice or are viewed by their supporters as a substitute for such major political battles. The evidence indicates that where committees have operated, the quality of debate in the Chamber and the acuteness of Question Time has increased and the strength of criticism voiced by MPs on these committees has in no way diminished.

The Chairman of the Parliamentary Labour Party, Mr. Houghton, has argued that "the backbencher is now mobilizing for an advance on the concentration of Ministerial and Executive power."[36] If this is to be successful, it must be an advance on many fronts, from looser discipline to better facilities for MPs, and one of the most important fronts, where major battles have been fought and will have to be won, is that of the specialist committees.

N O T E S

1. One was kept for Scottish legislation, the others being simply "A," "B," "C," as necessary.
2. 727 *H.C. Deb.,* 76.
3. 738 *H.C. Deb.,* 476–477.
4. This point was brought home to me when I went to press the case for better working conditions for MPs on the Leader of the House, Mr. Crossman. The latter replied "If I give you people desks, telephones, and secretaries, you will begin to think you are running something and believe me, you are not!"
5. Mr. Michael Foot, M.P., has often criticized the proposals for select committees. When I suggested (in 1968) that Mr. Foot's powerful attacks on the Government's policy, till November 1967, of keeping forces East of Suez, would have been helped if a Defense Committee had discovered all the costs and brought out the arguments between the service chiefs, Mr. Foot replied that "not knowing the

facts has never hampered me up to now, so I see no reason to change my views."

6. See the Prime Minister's speech at Stowmarket, July 3, 1964.

7. See S. A. Walkland, "Science and Parliament: The Orgins and Influence of the Parliamentary and Scientifice Committee I and II," in *Parliamentary Affairs*, XVII: 3 (Summer 1964), and by the same author "Science and Parliament: the Role of the Select Committees of the House of Commons," *ibid.*, XVIII: 3 (Summer 1965). Also N. J. Vig and S. A. Walkland, "Science Policy, Science Administration, and Parliamentary Reform," *ibid.*, vol. XIX.

8. See Arthur Palmer, M.P. (Chairman of the Committee), "The Select Committee on Science and Technology," *The Parliamentarian*, April 1969.

9. See Introduction to *United Kingdom Nuclear Reactor Programme, Report from the Select Committee on Science and Technology, 1966–67,* H.C. 381–XVII (1967).

10. Sir H. Legge-Bourke (Vice-Chairman of the Committee) in 765 *H.C. Deb.*, 963.

11. 291 *H.L. Deb.*, 1477–1549.

12. For a discussion of the content of the Report, see Roger Williams, "The Select Committee on Science and Technology," *Public Administration*, 46 (Autumn 1968).

13. 765 *H.C. Deb.*, 951–1072.

14. *Ibid.*, 968.

15. *Third Special Report of 1967–68,* No. 248 (May 9, 1968).

16. Mr. Ronald Butt in *The Power of Parliament* (2nd ed.) criticized the choice of subject on the grounds that the Government would scarcely have allowed itself to be influenced by the Committee's recommendations on such a critical subject (p. 375). This misunderstands the purpose of the Committee which never had any intention of influencing the Government in this fashion. But a major factor affecting the views of MPs and the public was the effect on farming, on the cost of living, and on the balance of payments of accepting the Common Agricultural Policy and on this the Government refused to disclose any information till the Committee insisted. After its Report these aspects of discussions in the House were far more acute and relevant.

17. *Report from the Select Committee on Agriculture, 1966–67, British Agriculture, Fisheries, and Food and the European Economic Community,* no. 378–XVII, vol. I (July 1967).

18. *Ibid.*, p. x.

19. 764 *H.C. Deb.*, 1135–1139.

20. *Ibid.*, 1118.

21. 754 *H.C. Deb.*, 260.

22. *Third Special Report from the Select Committee on Agriculture with Report from the Sub-Committee on Fisheries, 1967–68,* no. 309 (July 3, 1968).

23. *Report from the Select Committee on Agriculture, 1968–69,* no. 137 (February 12, 1969).

24. *Special Report from the Select Committee on Agriculture, 1968–69,* no. 138 (February 12, 1969).

25. *Third Special Report from the Select Committee on Education and Science, 1967–68,* no. 317 (July 9, 1968).

26. All these exchanges are pointed out in the *Third Special Report from the Select Committee on Education and Science, 1968–69,* no. 103 (January 28, 1969).

27. This was later described simply as The Committee on Overseas Aid.

28. H. Fairlie, *The Life of Politics,* p. 229.

29. *The Times,* leading article on April 29, 1968.

30. See for instances the speeches of Mr. J. Mendelsohn both before and after the Select Committee experiment in 669 *H.C. Deb.,* 240–248 and 788 *H.C. Deb.,* 1024–1032.

31. 738 *H.C. Deb.,* 485.

32. *Ibid.*

33. 765 *H.C. Deb.,* 968.

34. In interviews with the author in March 1969.

35. *First Report from the Select Committee on Procedure, 1968–69, Scrutiny of Public Expenditure and Administration,* no. 410 (July 23, 1969).

36. D. Houghton, "The Labour Backbenchers," *The Political Quarterly,* 40 (October 1969).

3

Reform of the Bundestag: The Case for General Debate

WILHELM HENNIS

In contrast to the House of Commons, parliaments on the continent of Europe have long used specialized committees. Specialization has gone so far in Germany that, in the opinion of some observers, it threatens the integrity of parliament. Proposals for reform, therefore, emphasize the value of the meeting of the whole house and the public deliberations which take place there. Wilhelm Hennis, one of the leading advocates of parliamentary reform among German political scientists, expresses the belief that public debate is parliament's distinctive function in the political process and deplores the failure of the German parliament to perform this function adequately. The difference between Mackintosh and Hennis is a difference in conception of the role of parliament in the political system, based on different national experiences with this institution.

Although there appears to be general agreement that the Bundestag continues to need reform, no consensus exists

This chapter is a revised, slightly condensed, and translated version of "Zur Rechtfertigung und Kritik der Bundestagsarbeit," which appeared originally in Horst Ehmke, Carlo Schmid, and Hans Scharoun, eds., *Festschrift für Adolf Arndt* (Frankfurt am Main: Europäische Verlagsanstalt, 1968). It is reprinted by permission of the author and publisher. The translation was prepared by Tamara Schoenbaum-Holtermann.

about the object of reforming it. Those who propose changes should be clear about what they wish to achieve, but they should also appreciate what a parliament can properly aspire to under modern circumstances. In view of the reforms that have been discussed and partially enacted within the last several years, it appears that there are two things in which many Members are interested. Some deplore Parliament's loss of status in comparison to executive institutions, and to them, restoration of parliamentary supremacy seems to be the primary goal of reforming the Bundestag. Others, partly in connection with this goal and partly quite independently of it, seek an improvement of parliamentary efficiency. As a result of the widespread view that the actual work of the Bundestag is done in committees, parliamentary parties, their working groups, and, not least, by the individual Member, these reform efforts concentrate on the improvement of the efficiency and working conditions of MPs and the groups into which they organize themselves. I would like to raise a few questions concerning these objectives.

MISCONCEIVED REFORM OBJECTIVES

To state it plainly, the demand for a restoration of parliamentary supremacy is based on a rather antiquated concept of our constitution. Drawing on the traditional continental doctrine of popular sovereignty, this concept assumes that the sovereign people have delegated their full power to the parliament which they elect. According to this school of thought, the doctrine of popular sovereignty is connected with the specifically continental interpretation of the doctrine of the separation of powers, which equates the cabinet exclusively with the executive. In this view, parliament should be the supreme decision-making body not only in lawmaking but also in determining basic policy. In spite of the chancellor's constitutional power to determine the guidelines of policy, this view holds that parliament should initiate and decide on basic policy, and the cabinet should merely carry it out. To be sure, the proponents of this school of thought are aware that in reality things are quite different, at least if the chancellor really governs, but they recognize this with dismay and consider it a deviation from the essential constitutional ideal.

The truth is that this concept of parliament as a supreme, sovereign body, sharing in the sacred sovereignty of the people, can be justified neither politically nor constitutionally but at best ideologically. A liberal constitution undoubtedly allocates specific authority, in the sense of responsibility, to the various governmental institutions, but this authority is never assigned exclusively to any one of them, with the exception of the administration of justice, which does not concern us here. This is true for all liberal constitutions which follow the tradition of the *constitutiones mixtae,* and it is true particularly of the parliamentary system of government. In this system, parliament has a share in matters within the cabinet's jurisdiction—in determining basic policy as well as appropriations—and, likewise, the cabinet participates fully in the lawmaking process. Even in those cases where parliament has the final word, as in appropriations and legislation, one cannot speak of parliament making final, sovereign decisions. Lawmaking, without the most thorough cooperation of both the cabinet responsible to parliament and the bureaucracy contributing its expertise, is neither conceivable nor desirable under modern conditions. Furthermore, parliament cannot claim an exclusive prerogative to exercise control over the cabinet or administration. Our whole system of government is based instead on a complicated, tightly interrelated set of checks and balances in which initiative, criticism, and decision-making are variously combined. There is no room in this system for the concept of a sovereign parliament.

It is of marginal historical interest to note that, up to the middle of the last century, such a concept was also completely foreign to the British; at best, it played a certain role during a limited transitional period as a polemic formula used by a bourgeois parliament in fighting the remains of the feudal-monarchic state. But in our age of radical democratization, the concept of a sovereign parliament cannot be reconciled with the realities of modern government. Any effort to restore the alleged former supremacy of parliament is bound to fail. In all functions of parliament, in lawmaking, in the supervision of bureaucracy, and even in the election of the chancellor, the Bundestag is no more than a participating institution; in the end it may be the one to decide —or, as the former Speaker of the Bundestag, Eugen Gerstenmaier, liked to say, it may "have the last word"—but what does that really signify, when this decision and this last word are predetermined by innumerable previous judgments and contributing factors?

It seems to me equally narrow-minded and, in the end, unconstructive, to concentrate the discussions of reform solely on an improvement of the Bundestag's working efficiency. As a rule, such objectives are based on a concept of work which is irrelevant to all political activity, and to parliamentary activity in particular, since it is a concept oriented to work in productive and technical enterprises. In an industrial society the Bundestag, too, is thought to be fully justified only if, like all other productive members of society, it has something to show for itself. But since the meeting of the whole house is suitable only for talking, and talking is a concept directly opposed to this concept of work, most discussions about an improvement of the Bundestag's efficiency leave the work of the plenary session out of account. Everyone familiar with working conditions in Bonn wishes the Members had better facilities in the Parliament House, including better secretarial service. But not every MP would know how to profit from better facilities. As anyone familiar with these things knows, it is quite pointless to let them all have secretaries and research assistants in equal measure.

If an improvement of efficiency is defined in terms of what parliament accomplishes in its committees and subcommittees, we should realize that everything it does there could also be done by other institutions. The polishing of legislative details and—*horribile dictu*—even lawmaking itself could be accomplished by a council of state composed of highly qualified experts on legislation, as long as the cabinet remains democratically responsible to the people. Parliament is not even absolutely necessary to supervise the bureaucracy. Everybody knows that parliamentary supervision has become merely a part of a much larger system of supervision. To be sure, no one who appreciates the blessings of a parliamentary system would like to live in a community in which parliament had no legislative or supervisory functions. What I want to point out is that so-called productive work is not the basic justification of parliamentary activity. But what is?

The Function of Debate

My thesis is that parliament as an institution can only be justified today by the activity which takes place on the floor of the house, even though this activity cannot be classified as work. But what does parliament actually accomplish in the meeting of the whole house? It seems to me that the greatest fault of all our discussions about the proper functions of parliament lies in the fact that in Germany we have no adequate concept either of the practical procedure or of the political meaning of what is accomplished on the floor of parliament. To date there is still only one theory in Germany of the function of the meeting of the whole house, namely that of Carl Schmitt. He claimed that parliament was justified only on the assumption that truth would result from public debate among free and independent representatives.[1] Since this concept influences even those critics of our present form of parliamentary activity, who are interested not only in an improvement of parliamentary efficiency but also in restoring parliament as a great forum of the nation, it is necessary to analyze it a little more closely.

It is surprising how a scholar who always prided himself on his sober judgment and detached observation could ever seriously have believed that a parliament—an assembly designated for political deliberations and decision-making—could be the ideal forum of free discussion, let alone one animated by a common search for the truth. Anyone entering a parliamentary chamber with such illusions will immediately realize that he is in the wrong place. This would certainly have been the case in the nineteenth, as well as in the twentieth century. As in so many things, Carl Schmitt mistook the dogmatic remarks of some French theoreticians, which had very little to do with real parliamentary activity, for the essence of the matter. The House of Commons, for one, has probably never seen any discussions in the sense of Schmitt's definition. In his novel *Phineas Finn,* Anthony Trollope has the liberal whip Barrington Erle define a concept of the duties of an MP which was no doubt typical for the time in which cabinet government began:

> He hated the very name of independence in Parliament, and when he was told of any man, that man intended to look to measures and not to men, he regarded that man as being both unstable as water and dishonest as the wind. No good could possibly come from such a one, and much evil might and probably would come. According to his theory of parliamentary government, the House of Commons should be divided by a marked line, and every member should be required to stand on one side of it or on the other. He thought that debates were good, because of the people outside, because they served to create that public opinion which was hereafter to be used in creating some future House of Commons; but he did not think it possible that any vote should be given on a great question, either this way or that, as the result of a debate; and he was certainly assured in his own opinion that any such changing of votes would be dangerous, revolutionary, and almost unparliamentary. A member's vote—except on some small crotchety open question thrown out for the amusement of crotchety members—was due to the leader of that member's party. Such was Mr. Erle's idea of the English system of Parliament, and, lending semi-official assistance as he did frequently to the introduction of candidates into the House, he was naturally anxious that his candidates should be candidates after his own heart.[2]

In this passage the purpose of parliamentary debates is accurately described: they are to influence public opinion, and thereby to determine the results of the next election. It should be remembered that this text was first printed in 1867, over a century ago, in the year of publication of Bagehot's *The English Constitution*.

This, however, does not yet explain what actually happens in parliamentary debates. Are those critics right who detect merely boring, self-righteous monologues and proclamations of unshakable points of view on the floor of the house? I am sure that anyone who listens a little more closely will easily find that in the great parliamentary debates neither a search for the truth nor a series of monologues takes place, but something much more interesting and more appropriate to political controversy. Debates constitute the pursuit of political competition by verbal means, in an attempt to expose one's opponents' weaknesses and to demonstrate one's own strength, leaving the final judgment to the electorate. This competition takes the form of trying to avoid discussion of those subjects raised by one's opponents and instead trying to force one's own favorite themes upon them. In this article, I am concerned only with parliamentary debates under a system having a relatively coherent majority and a sizable opposition. Nothing is less likely there than genuine discussion. What does go on, however—and what has gone on at times in the Bundestag at a high intellectual level—is the constant effort to force one's themes on one's opponents while evading theirs. The fact that neither one nor the other ever *quite* succeeds in this—just because the debate takes place before witnesses—represents the abiding justification of parliamentary debates. Measuring the political history of postwar Germany by the yardstick of parliamentary rhetoric, one might say that the political success of the center parties for the first two decades was shown in their success in forcing their favorite themes—Western integration and the free market economy—on the Social Democratic party (SPD), while the latter neither managed to state its own themes clearly nor to force them on its opponents. Toward the end of the 1960s things changed, first with respect to social problems and then with respect to educational policy. In these fields, the SPD undoubtedly succeeded in establishing the framework of discussion, foreshadowing its election victory of 1969.

The failure of the efforts of the Social Democrats to get in on policy-making while they were still in the opposition—efforts repeatedly made in the early 1960s—was entirely consistent with the parliamentary system as I conceive it. If the electorate determines not only the composition of parliament but also—as happened in Germany from 1953 to 1965—in effect determines the identity of the chancellor and his majority, it is consistent with democracy that this governing majority should strive, even in its rhetoric, to appear united and unshakable. The voters gave it a mandate; for the four-year term of parliament the majority is obliged to show what it can do. Without wanting to encourage the majority's stubbornness one did want it to be consistent. And if the opposition pointed to unkept campaign promises or demanded the fulfillment of the Government's program, it was only adjusting itself to the new situation.

In view of all this, what then is the sense of parliamentary debate? Its purpose is, above all, to force the Government, and, to a lesser extent, also the opposition, to justify their policy before the sovereign electorate. Parliamentary debate is not under the obligation to search for the truth, but is under the obligation to bring about justification and responsibility, which is no mean accomplishment. In modern parliamentary debates, one tries to force one's assumptions on the other side or to dispute the other's premises. Members of Parliament do not genuinely discuss with one another, but try to prove the weakness of their opponent's argument. Parliamentary debate is not a philosophical search for the truth but—how could it be anything else?—political contest by rhetorical means. It is a contest in which the issue is not power, but the justification for whatever position of power one happens to hold; it is the attempt to assume or assign responsibility before the public, especially before the voters. Modern parliamentary debate of this kind has an extremely important purpose. It compels politicians to produce rational justifications and public explanations for a given measure and against the alternative recommended by the opposition. Parliamentary debates, which usually take place after the really important decisions have already been made, and prior only to their final enactment, are not occasions for great initiatives in making policy, but rather for examining a proposed policy and the validity of the reasons for it.

Parliamentary debate thus becomes a guarantee of rational politics under modern conditions. One can be accountable only for one's reasons. Parliamentary debates are—or could be—the strongest protection against an increase in irrational decision-making in politics. In a democratic society, legal authority and power do not mean anything when it comes to justifying a specific measure, unless reasons are supplied to support the measure taken on the basis of this authority. No constitutionally established institution of government has the authority to make decisions without justifying them; all authority is tied to the obligation to give reasons and to account for its exercise. Responsibility can be demanded only after reasons have been given. Under modern conditions, responsibility, or being responsible, does not mean being subject to dismissal but being answerable for one's decisions. This does not preclude the possibility that parliamentary procedures requiring justification and the assignment of responsibility might occasionally result in the overthrow of a cabinet or the dismissal of a minister. Only, as a rule, such a result is not produced by a formal vote of no confidence but rather by the more or less free decision of the chancellor or the majority which supports him; the majority sacrifices the chancellor or the minister because it thinks that it can no longer be responsible for him, that is, answer for him publicly.

That is something which the SPD in the twenty years of its role as opposition party never fully understood. If I am right, the SPD believed that the Government had to justify itself and to be accountable to the opposition. Yet it is clear that the opposition, as an important part of our constitutional order, is not an end in itself but is justified only as it carries out its function on behalf of the electorate. The opposition forces the Government to justify its actions and assume responsibility, but it is not the addressee of these procedures; it only provokes them. It has been said that it is the function of the opposition to criticize, to supervise, and to propose alternative policies. However, it seems to me that, in view of the growing similarity of the policies proposed by the major parties, a more realistic account of the functions of the opposition would describe its role as compelling the Government to take responsibility for its actions and to justify them. An opposition which feels an urge to make itself heard and does not talk where the constitution says it should talk, namely on the floor of the house, an opposition, in other words, which does not initiate public procedures for justifying and taking responsibility, is worthless.

DEBATE IN THE BUNDESTAG

If we accept the premise that the floor of parliament is the place for justifying and assuming responsibility for policies, we must now ask to what extent the Bundestag has performed this function. If it has failed in this respect, major reform projects should begin here. There is no doubt that this is where reform is most needed.

Our rules of procedure prescribe three readings for the legislative process. It is not considered sufficient to justify a new law only once, but the procedures for justifying and taking responsibility are intended to be repeated before the public several times. Whether a bill is changed in the course of these procedures, as a result of criticism from the opposition or for whatever other reasons, has absolutely no relevance for the informative purpose of the three readings as such. No one requires that all the details and technicalities be dealt with during these public readings. But it seems reasonable to expect that parliament pass no bill, be it ever so technical, without at least a few words about the reasons for doing so. This applies also, or even more so, if the parties are of one opinion on a bill. For the objects of legislation, the citizen and the electorate, do not care whether the parties agree. Indeed, agreement among the parties rather arouses suspicion, unless the parties explain why they consider a certain measure right and worth passing.

If one examines the legislative work of the Bundestag by this standard, no words of criticism can, alas, be harsh enough. Anyone who reads the debates of the Bundestag will encounter strange remarks with which the Speaker frequently calls a bill up for a reading. Again and again, the transcript reads: "No debate is wanted," "Debate and explanation not requested," "The parties have agreed not to hold a debate," or, "The Federal Government deems it unnecessary to explain." After such a statement from the Speaker, a vote takes place immediately. The public does not learn what the Bundestag voted on, why there was a vote, or what could have been said for or against the bill. During the fourth term of the Bundestag, of the 429 bills enacted, fully 260 were not debated. Neither during the first, second, nor third readings, did the movers, the Government, the majority parties, or the opposition consider it necessary to say a word of justification, criticism, or anything about these bills. The most annoying aspect is that in the case of a considerable number of these bills, the transcript indicates opposing votes or abstentions, and yet it is impossible to find out why some MPs acted as they did. One might think that these 260 bills were of a purely technical nature, or at least that they hardly deserved to be justified. However, closer examination shows that this is not the case. There seems to be no correlation between the content of a bill and whether it is passed silently, debated for ten minutes, or, indeed, debated for three hours. Even on those bills which are debated, the transcript indicates the extreme reluctance of MPs to speak. Of the 429 bills enacted, 41 were debated for less than ten minutes; only 25 bills were debated for more than three hours on the floor of the house.

Not only does the intensity of Bundestag debates leave much to be desired but the manner of debating, too, hardly does justice to the demands of a modern democracy. If, under modern circumstances, the floor of the house is the place for justifying and assuming responsibility for policy, this should be reflected in the style of parliamentary speaking. If the public is the actual audience, MPs must speak in such a way that what is being discussed on the floor of the house directly attracts public attention. In short, parliamentary speeches must be directed out the window.

There have been significant differences between the CDU and the SPD in this regard. By and large, the CDU has understood the situation and has often exploited it skillfully, while for a long time the SPD missed the point pitifully. Adenauer's speeches, in particular, provided an excellent example. He embittered the SPD time and time again because he simply would not recognize the opposition as his partner in debate but addressed himself directly to the people. Even Schumacher, certainly a talented parliamentary politician, never understood the situation; as leader of the main opposition party he relentlessly and then bitterly demanded that the chancellor debate with him.

I do not want to be misunderstood as saying that I regard parliament as a forum for demagoguery and nothing more. No reasonable person would want to disparage the work which the Bundestag performs in its committees. Yet the style of discussion on the floor of the house must be distinguished from that in the committees and the working groups. If we want to maintain the public activity of parliament, then the style of parliamentary speaking must be adapted to the public. Besides, it is clear by now that, as a rule, it is neither possible nor desirable for the composition of the majority to change during a parliamentary term. On important issues, the minority is unable to persuade the majority on the floor of the house. Only the electorate can be persuaded, in anticipation of the next election. And this too should not be regarded as placing a premium on demagoguery. But the proceedings in the public sessions of parliament must be regarded as a permanent election campaign, if the real decision remains with the electorate. And this is precisely what it ought to be, for only under these conditions can parliament perform the function of informing the electorate.

The political parties in Germany have not yet fully understood the opportunities which parliamentary debates offer them. They still believe that the decision of the voters can only be affected during election campaigns, that voters do not perceive what goes on in parliament, and that parliamentary activity therefore need not be made palatable to them. Actually, all empirical research on voting behavior indicates that changes in electoral opinion take place very slowly and hardly ever as the result of an election campaign. If the parties complain that their meager financial resources prevent them from adequately informing the public, one cannot be too emphatic in pointing out to them the possibilities inherent in parliamentary debate. We know, of course, that the times are long past when the great newspapers would publish full-page parliamentary reports. No one today would read them. But if parliamentary debates were to be conducted in a manner which corresponds to the new political situation, there is no doubt that the press and the public would be far more attentive than they are. If MPs complain that the German press takes little notice of the Bundestag, they should find fault not with the press but first of all with themselves. A parliament which holds as few public sessions as the Bundestag cannot claim the right to be a frequent object of newspaper reporting. And since the style of most of today's parliamentary debates is so little directed to the public, the press cannot be reproached for its inability to report the proceedings.

On examining the German literature on parliamentary government in this century with a view to discovering how the institution of parliament has been justified, one encounters only the writings of Max Weber. For Weber the main justification of parliamentary procedures lay in their contribution to the recruitment of political leaders. He thought that the floor of the house performed a function in recruiting leaders which could not be performed anywhere else so effectively, so publicly, and in a manner so directly permitting popular judgment. Whatever the shortcomings of the House of Commons may be, none of its critics has ever contested that it still fulfills this function. To this day the debates in the House of Commons offer each new generation of politicians a chance to make good. To this day, the rhetorical mastery of difficult matters determines advancement in the political hierarchy. If, in a modern democracy, the recruitment of leaders is the function of the political parties, these have the obligation to perform this function as openly as possible. Since the public does not take part in nominating parliamentary candidates, at least it should be allowed to witness the process of advancement within parliament. Unfortunately, the Bundestag fails in this respect too. This failure results from the lamentable practice by which a small oligarchy of MPs dominates the debates.

The life of parliament is endangered by an exclusivity of participation in debates, which the following figures, based on the fourth term of the Bundestag, reveal: CDU, 251 Members, of whom 19 (8%) gave 422 of 1216 speeches (34%); SPD, 203 Members, of whom 23 (11%) gave 667 of 1281 speeches (52%); FDP, 67 Members, of whom 11 (16%) gave 307 of 618 speeches (50%). This monopolization of debating time, which is particularly marked in the SPD, hinders the development of a capable younger generation of MPs and, at the same time, stifles the interest of all Members in what transpires on the floor. An MP who does not have the slightest chance of being recognized to speak and who has heard what is being said on the floor in preparatory party caucuses can only be moved to attend the sessions of the house by pure reverence for his leaders.

Indignation about these Bundestag practices is widespread, and that is a good thing. Parliamentary reform will not be set in motion by professorial preaching. It will be brought about only if its goals impress those concerned as political necessities. After the election of September 1969, the SPD succeeded in forming a Government on the basis of a very narrow majority produced by a coalition with the FDP. In the long run the SPD will have to recognize, as the CDU/CSU has now recognized, that its capacity to govern as well as its capacity to conduct a coherent opposition depends on receiving an unequivocal mandate from the electorate. The parliamentary floor leaders who, for all practical purposes, control the course of the debates will have to recognize that their rigid planning of debates hurts their parties more than it helps them.

The future development of the Bundestag will greatly depend on the performance of individual Members of Parliament. This is an indication of weakness in the institutionalization of the Bundestag. A lot will also depend on the official staff of the Bundestag, and in particular on its director. It is to their persistent efforts that we owe the small reforms of the last few years. In the end, perhaps even scholarship can make its modest contribution. Above all, it can resolutely defy the use of outdated, nineteenth-century constitutional norms to obstruct the working of the parliamentary system of government which Germany has finally achieved.

NOTES

1. When he found that modern parliaments could not perform this function, Schmitt decided that they were obsolete [*Ed.*].
2. Anthony Trollope, *Phineas Finn* (London: World's Classics edition, 1962), pp. 18 ff.

4

Parliament under the Fifth French Republic: Difficulties of Adapting to a New Role

FRANÇOIS GOGUEL

The desire to enhance the role of parliament in the political system motivates most proposals for parliamentary reform in Great Britain and Germany. Although conceptions of the proper role of parliament differ, they all presuppose the desirability of increasing the influence of the institution. By contrast, the controversy in France turns on the basic question of parliamentary power. In the selection below, François Goguel, a distinguished French political scientist and Secretary-General of the Senate, the upper house of Parliament, expresses the view that the Constitution of 1958 established a better balance of power between parliament and the executive than had previously existed. If there has been a decline of parliament under this new constitution, Goguel believes that it is due to the failure of the National Assembly to adapt to its new constitutional position.

Seen from the outside, the French political system today is very similar to that of the beginning of the twentieth cen-

This chapter is a revision of a paper originally presented at a Conference on the Future of the Legislative Power, Princeton University, April 1966. It is printed here by permission of the author.

tury. There is now, as then, a President, head of state, not politically responsible, elected for seven years. He appoints the Government, which is responsible to a Parliament composed, as formerly, of two houses. The lower house, elected by universal suffrage, was called the Chamber of Deputies until 1940. Since 1946 it has been known as the National Assembly.

It would appear that there are two major differences between the Fifth and Third Republics: instead of being elected by a joint session of the two houses of Parliament, the President is elected by universal suffrage; instead of having powers absolutely identical to those of the popularly elected National Assembly, the Senate no longer has full legislative power. Specifically, the National Assembly can "have the last word" in the drawing up of bills and the Senate does not have the right to express a lack of confidence in the Government. The most important of these changes, the one whose effects on the nature and extent of the legislative power are obviously the greatest, is the fact that instead of being elected by the Parliament, the President is now elected by universal suffrage. It is obvious that he therefore determines and directs the policy of the nation to a far greater extent than previously. But if the anatomy of the French political system—that is, the structure of its basic institutions—has undergone only slight changes, the physiology—that is, the way in which they function—has been deeply transformed.

CONSTITUTIONAL INNOVATIONS

The legislative competence of the houses, their internal organization, and the rules of procedure governing their debates, have, since 1958, been established by the Constitution. This is entirely new and limits their freedom of action to a great extent.

The scope of the legislative power of Parliament was formerly defined by precedent. Apart from a few exceptions instituted by a law of August 17, 1948, a legal text could be changed only by a law enacted by Parliament and a new law could practically always supersede an executive decree. Today the Constitution (article 34) defines the "domain of the law" and has created efficient mechanisms which enable the Government to insure that the line drawn between its domain and that of Parliament is respected.

The result is that the number of laws—that is, the number of legal acts voted by Parliament—has been considerably reduced since 1958 by comparison with former periods. From 1947 to 1954 (when a partial revision of the 1946 Constitution occurred) there were on the average 255 laws per year. From 1955 to 1957, during the last three years of the Fourth Republic, there were on an average 175—that is, their number had already decreased by a third. From February 4, 1959, to July 1, 1968, Parliament voted 815 laws or, on the average, a bit more than 85 per year. But the comparison of these bare figures is misleading. Under the Fourth Republic it was usual for 80 or 100 laws to be voted each year practically without being discussed by either house. They agreed on the text almost immediately because these texts gave no cause for controversy. Such laws still exist under the Fifth Republic but it is principally in this category that there are fewer legislative texts each year. Article 34 has not really taken from Parliament what was most important in its legislative power.

However, it must also be remembered that Parliament is no longer the only lawmaking body. Article 11 of the Constitution enables the President to submit certain bills directly to the people, by means of a referendum. Article 16 furthermore enables the President, in exceptional circumstances, to exercise the legislative power himself. This article was applied in 1961, after the coup d'etat undertaken in Algiers by General Salan, and sixteen presidential "decisions" with the force of law were taken by virtue of this provision. Article 38 of the Constitution enables Parliament to delegate legislative power to the Government temporarily, permitting the Government to take measures within this delegated jurisdiction by decree. This is not, in fact, a new procedure: the Third Republic had known a similar procedure of "decree-law" *(décrets-loi)* in 1926, then from 1934 to 1940. The Fourth Republic had rapidly found the means of re-establishing this procedure, despite a poorly phrased constitutional prohibition. In sum, while Parliament enacted 815 statutes in the first decade of the Fifth Republic, 131 legislative acts were promulgated without the participation of Parliament.[1]

The Government also finds itself much better equipped than formerly to obtain votes in accordance with its wishes from the parliamentary assemblies, thanks to the changes in the procedure of legislative debates introduced by the 1958 constitution. The number of permanent committees in each Assembly has been reduced to 6 (against 19 at the end of the Fourth Republic); their role has been limited to the presentation of amendments to Government bills, which the houses used to discuss, not in their original text, but in the text established by the committee. The traditional principle according to which "the house is always master of the agenda" has been abrogated and the right to establish the agenda has been given to the Government. The right of amendment has been granted to Ministers. The Government has been empowered to oppose consideration of parliamentary amendments which have not first been submitted to the competent committee. Finally, the Government has been given the right to require the houses to decide by a single vote on all or part of a text under discussion, incorporating only those amendments which the Government accepts.

Furthermore, the evolution started in 1920 by the Chamber of Deputies' vote of a rule of procedure restricting parliamentary initiative in financial affairs, which continued under the Fourth Republic, was crowned in 1958 by the absolute suspension of all parliamentary financial initiative. There is an absolute prohibition on motions creating or increasing public expenditures or diminishing revenues, whether these are introduced by a Member of Parliament or by a parliamentary committee.

Last of all, the measures taken by decree-laws in 1956, reorganizing the procedure governing budget debates, limiting the length of debate, and rendering the tabling and the passing of parliamentary amendments more difficult, have been reintroduced and made precise by the Constitution of 1958. Indeed, this document provides a procedure which has never been applied: the Government may even promulgate the yearly budget by decree if Parliament has not reached a definite decision, even a negative one, within a time-limit of 70 days after the tabling of the budget bill.

We have here a set of constitutional prescriptions whose application Parliament is forced to accept because of the control exercised by the Constitutional Council over the drafting of the rules of the parliamentary assemblies. Their effect is to make the position of the Government during debates considerably stronger than it was under the Third or Fourth Republics. This implies a corresponding weakening of the power of the Members of the Assemblies to impose their will on the Government.

The new rules concerning the conditions in which the Government can request a vote of confidence during a legislative debate have the same effect. The existence of a nearly unconditional right of dissolution in the hands of the President constitutes the final element in the pattern of the Government's strength vis-à-vis the Assembly. The threat of dissolution during a debate on a motion of censure is indeed very often sufficient to induce a certain number of deputies, not really in favor of the Government but even less desirous of facing the voters, to reject the censure.

The present organization and exercise of the lawmaking power, in comparison with that existing before 1958, shows that the Fifth Republic is not only characterized by the development of presidential power but also by the limitation of parliamentary power. Nevertheless, at least in certain respects, the development begun in 1958 has simply been an accentuation of an evolution started much earlier. The Fifth Republic has generalized, extended, and reinforced an evolution of the structure of parliamentary power which had begun before 1958 in a fragmentary but nonetheless significant fashion. The disadvantages of a situation in which Parliament, and more particularly, the National Assembly, were given responsibilities which they were incapable of performing satisfactorily, had become obvious during the Fourth Republic.

In the minds of the members of the Constituent Assemblies of 1945–1946, the National Assembly was not only to exercise the legislative power. It was also its task to decide on the nation's policy and to participate closely in the formation of the Government charged with carrying out this policy. Hence a mechanism had been instituted to invest the Premier and to approve his program *before* he could officially be appointed by the President of the Republic. The conditions under which the Government could be called to account before the Assembly had been minutely regulated by the Constitution in the hope of reducing the number of ministerial crises. But, in fact, these overcomplicated rules were twisted in such a way that the great majority of Governments during the Fourth Republic fell under conditions which did not conform to the prescriptions of the Constitution. Finally, a legislative procedure had been established by the Assembly itself which, except in financial matters, had the effect of constantly putting the Government in a weak position by promoting the maximum number of parliamentary initiatives.

The effects of this system of parliamentary sovereignty were bad. The Fourth Republic was a period of great cabinet instability: 20 cabinets in 11 years and 5 months, during which the total duration of ministerial crises—that is, periods between the fall of one Government and the nomination of its successor—exceeded a year. During the last year in which this system operated—from May 1957 to May 1958—the duration of such crises was 89 days, almost one out of four days. As Philip Williams has shown, ministerial crises had become an indispensable element in the working of the French political system, because they were the only way of forcing the different political parties to come to an agreement on a policy. But this agreement was always short-term, questioned each time a new problem arose.

The most urgent Government bills were only adopted after long debates and substantial modifications of their initial provisions. These difficulties had led to the revival of decree-law despite the constitutional provision intended to abolish them. By this means temporary delegations of legislative power became possible and all cabinets used them from 1953 onward. The weakening of the Government's authority was soon extended overseas—where the most difficult problems France had to resolve arose—by the de facto independence of French governors and residents. The consequences were particularly serious in North Africa and, indeed, how could it be otherwise when in Paris neither the Government nor the Parliament managed to determine the means by which their policy could be carried out? The debate in the National Assembly in June 1952 on policy toward Tunisia had clearly illustrated this weakness. Seven motions were successively refused, and the debate ended without any positive conclusion.

It was obvious to all that the disordered state of the French political system was due to the existence of the practically unlimited sovereignty of Parliament established in 1946. It is therefore not surprising that the majority of political parties—with the sole exception of the Communist party and a fraction of the Socialist party—accepted the establishment of a regime in 1958 which provided for a better division of labor between Government and Parliament, that is to say, a limitation of parliamentary power while maintaining the fundamental principle of a parliamentary system, that of the political responsibility of the Government to the National Assembly. In the practice of the first decade of the Fifth Republic, however, this regime came to look very different from the way it was envisaged in the beginning, and the role of Parliament became even less important than imagined by many of those who had initially accepted the 1958 Constitution.

CONSTITUTIONAL PRACTICE

Formally, the maintenance of a parliamentary regime in France can be verified by the fact that the Government is politically responsible to the National Assembly and has fairly frequently requested a vote of confidence from it. But in actual fact the French political regime has undergone a profound transformation because the Government does not consider the different political currents which exist in Parliament as a basic factor in its decisions. According to the expression used by General de Gaulle in the speech he made in Bayeux on June 16, 1946, the Government no longer "proceeds" from the National Assembly but from the President of the Republic. With the President presiding over its meetings as the Council of Ministers, the Government has become the executive organ of a policy conceived mainly by the President of the Republic. Its role is to apply this policy and, in particular, to obtain from Parliament the adoption of legislative and financial measures necessary for its application.

There has been a complete change in the balance of power. The President of the Republic is no longer merely an arbiter, intervening in political life in times of serious difficulties between Parliament and Government, as he was initially conceived. Rather, it is from him that the policy impetus comes. He concerns himself with policy details more or less according to the nature of the problems. Until July 1968, foreign policy and defense policy, the policy of decolonization, and that adopted toward Algeria during the first years of the Fifth Republic, occupied his attention more completely than economic, financial, and social policies or administrative reforms. But all things considered, no domain of government activity escapes his initiative and his control. His mode of election was modified in 1962, by the substitution of universal suffrage for the special college of local government representatives instituted in 1958, to legitimate this widening of his role. As a result of his direct election by all the citizens, it is understandable that the views on Government policy prevailing in the National Assembly, elected under the same conditions, have no greater influence than his.

During the parliamentary term of 1958–1962, the majority on which the Government had to rely in the National Assembly was far from homogeneous. Added to the Gaullists (UNR), most of whose members always upheld the Government, the majority included the Popular Republicans (MRP) and the Independents. Nonetheless, in the numerous circumstances in which it appeared clear that the policy of the Government did not correspond to the wishes of the majority of the deputies, either with regard to domestic problems (most often of an economic nature) or with regard to defense policy or international policy, the Assembly for four years avoided direct conflict with a Government nominated by the President of the Republic and conducting a policy inspired or upheld by him.

Moreover, no conflict arose between the Government and the National Assembly during the Parliament of 1962–1967, in which the Government had a disciplined majority. The latter was composed of the Gaullists (UNR-UDT) group and of the group of Independent Republicans, that is, those conservatives favoring the Fifth Republic and the policy of the President of the Republic. The problem of the relationship between the Assembly and the Government shifted; it was no longer solved in public, but rather in private meetings during which the Ministers and the Members of the majority agreed in advance on amendments to Government bills. This situation, which removed all uncertainty from the results of the National Assembly's deliberations, did not necessarily mean a lessening of parliamentary influence on the terms of legislation. But it was obviously discouraging for the opposition, and its most important leaders hardly participated in the Assembly's debates.

It seemed, on balance, that the existence in the National Assembly of a disciplined, coherent majority—almost unprecedented in French political history—disconcerted all the actors in the parliamentary drama. It led the opposition to abandon its role, for it seemed useless to its leaders to express their views in detail in the National Assembly. They knew they would not be able to bring a wavering faction of the majority over to their side and thus open a ministerial crisis or at least create serious difficulties for the Government. This led the Government to conceive its relationship with Parliament in terms of producing a compromise among the points of view expressed within the groups of the majority of the National Assembly and to neglect entirely what was done and said in the Senate.

But it would be wrong to conclude from this state of affairs that Parliament no longer plays any part in French political life, for everything finally rests on the existence in the National Assembly of a majority faithful to the President of the Republic and to the Government charged by the President with carrying out the policy he determines.

THE REASONS FOR THE DECLINE OF PARLIAMENT

Michel Debré, who was one of the principal authors of the 1958 constitution and who, as Prime Minister, had a major part in putting it into force, undoubtedly intended to institute a parliamentary system in France—a renovated parliamentary system, to be sure, one in which the long-standing sovereignty of the National Assembly would be ended and in which the Government would no longer be subordinated to Parliament, yet nonetheless a system in which Parliament would play a great role and take an active part in the control of Government policy. Why has reality not fulfilled these intentions? How is it that the system has so rapidly become one in which, by and large, Parliament appears as a secondary element? The answer to this question is not straightforward, for this evolution has resulted from a variety of factors differing in nature and in importance.

One of the first, one of the most important, is undoubtedly the character and the actions of General de Gaulle as they resulted not only from his personality but also from the circumstances in which, after June 18, 1940, he exercised political power for the first time. Since his return to public office in 1958 had been successively approved by Parliament in June and by the electorate in the September referendum, he could obviously not consider that his rise to the Presidency was merely the result of the vote of the college of notables provided by the new constitution. It was not conceivable that having become President, he should assume the role of a mere figurehead and from time to time that of an arbiter between Government and Parliament. On January 8, 1959, the official communiqué in which the President announced that Debré had been named Prime Minister, after having "submitted for the approval" of General de Gaulle "the composition and the program" of the cabinet he proposed to form, already showed clearly the change that had taken place in the role of chief of state. "Proceeding" from the President, deliberating exclusively under his chairmanship, the Government was obviously going to find itself so closely associated with him that parliamentary criticism of the Government would appear to be equally directed against the President. One of the main elements of the classic parliamentary regime, a nonpolitical chief of state, was lacking under the Fifth Republic from the beginning.

But another reason, no doubt as important, explains why, from the very first months of 1959, Parliament did not fully exercise the powers which it did have under the Constitution; it is simply that it did not want to exercise them in the area in which they were most onerous, that is, in the Algerian problem. Knowing how difficult this problem was, that it had caused the overthrow of the Fourth Republic, and aware also of the confidence the public in both France and in Algeria had in General de Gaulle's capacity to solve this problem, an undoubted majority of the Members of Parliament decided more or less consciously to leave Algerian policy to the President. During a debate in October 1959, after de Gaulle's speech concerning self-determination, the spokesman of the left-wing opposition groups explicitly declared that they had no intention of doing anything which could "upset the carrying out of the Algerian policy defined by the President." This acknowledged the President's right not only to determine the nation's policy in an essential field but also to implement it. In February 1960, after the "week of the barricades" in Algiers, when the Government asked Parliament for a delegation of legislative power so that it could take the necessary measures to meet the situation this uprising had revealed, it was on the initiative of an MRP deputy that the National Assembly specified that these decrees should be signed by "General de Gaulle, the President of the Republic." In fact, this signature would have been needed in any case under article 13 of the Constitution. But this amendment clearly had a political significance: the Assembly left the Algerian policy more willingly to the President, who was not constitutionally responsible to it, than to the Government, which was. Thus the National Assembly renounced its control, in the true sense of the word, over a then fundamental element of the nation's policy.

By concentrating its activities on problems such as veterans' pensions, grants to parochial schools, the fixing of agricultural prices, and the road building program—that is, on problems supposed to be electorally profitable—while refusing to deal actively with the Algerian problem, the Parliament of the first years of the Fifth Republic contributed to lessening its own prestige and to decreasing the role it played in governing.

When in June 1962 a majority of deputies signed an unofficial but public declaration in which they condemned the foreign policy of the Government nominated by General de Gaulle (while during the same and the following month, on two occasions, it was impossible to mobilize the same majority to support a motion of censure) a new step was taken in the process of self-abdication by which the National Assembly shirked the responsibilities incumbent upon it under a parliamentary regime.

The explanation of this attitude lies no doubt in the fact that the vast majority of deputies belonging to the traditional political parties at first considered the Fifth Republic to be a temporary regime. A certain number of politicians more or less deliberately followed what has been called the "submarine" tactic: they participated as discreetly as possible in parliamentary life so that they might surface again after the end of the Algerian war without running the risk of suffering personally from the critical reaction to the Algerian settlement which they expected from the public.

From the very first parliamentary term, it was also clear that the procedures provided in the Constitution to permit MPs to compel the Government to justify its policies publicly would not assume their intended importance. It seems that an old French parliamentary habit prevailed: only those debates are regarded as important which launch an attack on the Government. Thus, the deputies were unable to adapt to a regime which precluded such debates except on motions of censure.

Members of Parliament—especially those in opposition but also occasionally members of the majority—often complained that the Government used its power to fix the agenda to prevent the discussion of private members' bills. It is true that the proportion of bills voted on governmental initiative was very high: between 1959 and 1968, it was just under 90 percent of the total.[2] But few private members' bills are the object of a committee report, without which they cannot be put on the agenda. And it must be noted that if the houses really wanted to establish a complementary agenda to be added to the Government's priority agenda, they could easily do so by deciding to sit on Mondays and Saturdays in addition to their normal sittings which take place from Tuesday to Friday.

It would also be possible for them to develop an efficient supervision of governmental activity by deciding, as they have the right to, upon the creation of temporary committees to examine the administrative, financial, and technical management of government services. But during the first decade of the Fifth Republic only two commissions of this type were established.

By and large one has the impression that there has been practically no effort on the part of Parliament to adapt itself to the new modes of activity resulting from the Constitution. The loss of its former means of pressure on the Government has demoralized certain of its Members. Convinced that under the new regime they no longer have any means of influencing the Government's policy, they remained passive. Hence the absenteeism that can often be noted during the sittings of the houses and a similar absenteeism at committee meetings.

A sort of vicious circle had become established: convinced that they could do little to influence the general policy of the

Government because of the provisions of the Constitution and the existence of a disciplined majority, the Members of Parliament did not fully use the powers at their disposal. As a result the Government's independence vis-à-vis the Parliament increased year by year.

It may be, however, that a better equilibrium between the role of the President of the Republic and the Government, on the one hand, and that of Parliament, on the other, has been achieved. The resignation of General de Gaulle on April 28, 1969, after the defeat of the referendum on the reform of the Senate and the creation of regions, confirmed the democratic character of a regime in which the authority of the President is accompanied by his responsibility to the electorate. The election of Georges Pompidou to succeed him demonstrated the attachment of public opinion to the institutions of the Fifth Republic and led the opposition to weaken appreciably it attacks against the regime, whose legitimacy it recognizes today more clearly than ever before. Contrary to the attitude which they adopted from 1962 to 1969, the Communist and Socialist members of the executive committee *(bureau)* of each house now take part in the protocol visits which these committees traditionally pay to the President of the Republic.

As a result of the elections of 1967 and 1968, the Government's majority in Parliament had been enlarged. Several leaders of the center groups in the National Assembly supported the candidacy of Georges Pompidou for the Presidency of the Republic and, after his election, entered the Government of Jacques Chaban-Delmas which he had appointed. The fact that the new Prime Minister had been President of the National Assembly for more than ten years had more than symbolic value. After June 1969 there were changes in the relations between Government and Parliament. The "package vote" procedure, for example, under which the Government can compel a house to act by a single vote on all or part of a bill, including only those amendments which the Government accepts, was used neither in the course of the brief debates of June 1969, nor in the course of the special session of September, nor in the course of the first weeks of the regular session of autumn 1969. To be sure, the Government may not always be able to avoid using this procedure, for the policy which it considers necessary may arouse the opposition of its majority. Certain aspects of its reform program do not correspond to the views of the conservative majority—even on the Gaullist benches—which was elected in 1968 in reaction to the strikes and demonstrations of May and June of that year. However, the President and the Prime Minister both clearly wanted to give evidence of respect for Parliament. This obviously does not mean that Parliament will resume the role which it proved incapable of playing under the Fourth Republic, but it can mean that its Members will exercise their legislative role and their function of controlling governmental activity more completely than before.

It is not conceivable that these changes will restore the political initiative to the National Assembly which it had before 1958 and which, in today's world, a parliamentary assembly is incapable of exercising properly. But it is possible that these changes will arrest the decline of the role of Parliament which was evident in France until the spring of 1969.

NOTES

1. Of these, 78 were made under article 38 of the Constitution and 53 under the law approved by referendum on April 8, 1962, after the Evian agreements on Algerian independence.
2. For the first decade of the Fifth Republic the figure was 88.6 percent, but it was declining toward the end of this period. It was 93.1 percent between 1959 and 1962; 87.4 percent between 1962 and 1967; and 79.3 percent from 1967 to 1968.

5 *Parliament under the Fifth French Republic: Patterns of Executive Domination*

PHILIP WILLIAMS

The distribution of power between Government and parliament has been controversial throughout modern French political history. Although François Goguel, in the previous chapter, expresses the belief that the present French constitution provides a suitable balance between executive and legislative power to which parliament only needs to adapt itself more effectively, Philip Williams, in the essay below, asserts that parliament has recently suffered from excessive executive domination. Williams, who wrote the definitive study of French politics under the Fourth Republic, attributes the decline of parliament under the Fifth Republic both to constitutional changes unduly favoring the executive and to political changes which provided French Governments in the 1960s and 70s with unexpected and unprecedented parliamentary majorities. He criticizes the extent to which French executives have exercisd their new constitutional and political prerogatives and charges them with violating the spirit of parliamentary government. The difference of opinion between Goguel and Williams reflects the unsettled controversy over the proper balance between Government and parliament in France, a controversy which regained practical importance when de Gaulle's resignation removed his exceptional personal influence from the scales.

THE INFLUENCE OF THE BACKBENCHER

In the National Assembly the influence of the majority on the Government gives Parliament a real political importance which

This chapter is a revision of a paper originally presented at a Conference on the Future of the Legislative Power, Princeton University, April 1966. It is printed here by permission of the author.

97

is neglected by public opinion because the influence is mainly exercised behind the scenes. But the deputies who oppose the Government are not only confronted by the barrier of ministerial authority but lack any power over the organization of the house itself and are therefore unable (as well as unwilling) to play the part expected of a vigorous parliamentary opposition.

While during its first term, between 1959 and 1962, the National Assembly resounded with frequent and bitter complaints against the Government from the mouths of its own supporters, these grievances were not repeated. The situation had been transformed by the end of the Algerian war, the appointment of a less intransigent personality as Prime Minister, and the Gaullist victory at the election of 1962, repeated narrowly in 1967 and emphatically in 1968. In the Assembly there was a loyal majority which, like disciplined majority parties in other countries, frequently criticized and sought to influence the Government but in the last resort accepted its decisions and voted for them with impressive discipline. In turn, and in consequence, the Government showed more confidence in its supporters and paid more attention to them than it had previously.

There are many ways in which the active Gaullist deputy can seek to influence the policy of a minister. If his object is to draw attention to a problem which has not yet come before Parliament, he can work through the study group of the parliamentary party concerned with the particular subject. Perhaps he can persuade it to prepare a bill which he then can urge the Gaullist parliamentary party to put forward in the name of the majority, or—if the Minister is sympathetic—he can use the study group to press his proposals on the Government in the hope that it will become part of the cabinet's program. When a question is already under discussion he can, if his views commend themselves to other members of his party, urge them on the member of the executive committee with whom he is in touch and try to have them raised at the weekly meeting of the Gaullist parliamentary party in the Salle Colbert. Alternatively he can work through the appropriate legislative committee, where the President and the *rapporteur* [reporter] will both belong to the majority and, much more often than not, to the Gaullist group. He can try directly to persuade the Minister. If he fails, he can appeal to the executive committee and the party meeting. And if discontent with the Government's measure or policy is widespread in the Assembly, the Member (and especially the *rapporteur)* will often find that the mood of discontent affects the Independent Republicans; until 1968 this could threaten the Government's majority. The relative autonomy of these allies may irritate the "unconditionals," but it sometimes provides a useful channel to indicate the uneasiness of the deputies, even Gaullist ones.

These opportunities are not merely theoretical. Especially from its second term, the Assembly showed that pressure from the majority could lead the Government to introduce a bill, like the amnesty for political offenders which it refused in November 1964 and presented in December; or modify one before putting it to Parliament, like the law on the public broadcasting and television service or the bill introducing the value-added tax; or amend one in the house, like the pensions code reform or the bill establishing the State Security Court; or postpone and amend one, like the statute for conscientious objectors; or withdraw and improve one, like the bill on the resettlement of refugees from North Africa. No doubt many of these measures were of secondary importance, the Government's concessions were sometimes quite minor, and, naturally, the influence of the deputies was not necessarily exercised in a desirable direction. Nevertheless Parliament, and in particular the majority in the Assembly, plays a much greater part in the legislative process than the public realizes. This is because the influence is nearly always exercised in private, and public disputes like that over the value-added tax are rare events. The new situation is so contrary to the whole French parliamentary tradition that neither press nor public has yet adjusted to it, while the Gaullists themselves are proud of their own unity and discipline, anxious to conceal their internal disputes, and in consequence not eager to draw attention to it. Indeed it is a sign of the difficulty of adaptation that so few Frenchmen seem to realize that the "unconditional" public discipline of the majority, which they mock and criticize, is the necessary foundation for the governmental stability which the same people prize.

THE BRITISH SYSTEM MISTRANSLATED

Michel Debré took his model from the British House of Commons, but he did not believe that the French electorate would ever, like the British, return a solid party majority. He therefore tried to invent formal rules and restrictions to achieve by procedural means the results which in Britain are the consequence of party discipline. He was convinced that rigid restraints were needed to cure the deputies (not the senators) of their obsession with the making and unmaking of Governments to the exclusion of, or rather as a substitute for, every other parliamentary function. Unfortunately Debré's devoted admiration for the British constitution was matched only by his systematic misunderstanding of it. He seemed unaware that on 28 days in every session the opposition is free to choose the subject of debate, and of course to insist, if it wishes, on a vote at the end. But Debré denied not only any right to vote on motions proposed by the opposition (for understandable reasons) but also the right to vote on the Government's own declarations of policy (except with its authority). His ground was that the House of Commons votes very rarely; but it does so three times as often as the National Assembly today. In Britain, taxes are temporarily authorized by resolution of the Commons on the day the budget is introduced, but the House later discusses it for several weeks. Yet when deputies complained that they had too little time to discuss the budget properly (and admittedly it had taken far too long in the past), Debré replied that in Britain the House of Commons passes the budget in a single afternoon. It is a pity he never took his own advice to the complaining Members, whom he urged to "spend the next recess comparing your powers with those of members of the British House of Commons."

In fact, the Gaullist leaders, in their natural desire to restrain the deputies by procedural means from harassing the Government, have gone far to restrain them also from exercising those parliamentary functions which the House of Commons still performs: first, the function of persuading the Government to change its mind, either by argument or by an appeal to public opinion outside; second, the function of persuading the electorate to return a new Government at the next election. These restraints were understandable in the crisis years of the first National Assembly, when the Government had no reliable majority and an assertive Parliament might merely have produced an insoluble crisis by obstructing de Gaulle over Algeria without being able to provide an alternative. But in the Parliaments elected in 1962, 1967, and 1968, with a loyal Gaullist majority and no external crisis, the Government used its immense powers no differently. For first the Government took for itself a formidable arsenal of powers to serve as a *substitute* for a majority. Then the Gaullists acquired a majority, which should have allowed the Government —assuming it really wanted an effective Parliament—to use its arsenal of powers with prudence and moderation. Not a bit of it. It has taken full advantage of both its political and procedural strength so as to ensure that the all-out opposition has few opportunities to appeal to the country and the moderate opposition exercises no influence on policy.

For the losers from the new regime, however justified the reproach that they might have adapted better, are not the sole authors of their own misfortunes. The Government, which gains from it, has exploited its advantages at every point to the great detriment of the prospects of an effective parliamentary system. Let me give three examples of this proposition. First, the way the Government uses it control over the parliamentary timetable.

Second, the failure of oral question day. Third and principally, the procedure for amending legislation through parliamentary discussion.

THE INSTRUMENTS OF GOVERNMENT DOMINATION

First, the parliamentary timetable. In the Fourth Republic this was managed with extreme inefficiency; the house always insisted on keeping control of its business and frequently made last-minute changes, postponing essential but disagreeable Government business in order to discuss some popular Private Member's proposal. In the Fifth Republic the Government enjoys complete priority, except on oral question day, for the business it puts down. Many people, including me, thought at the time that this was clearly an improvement since Parliament had plainly proved incapable of organizing its own timetable effectively; it has been disappointing to see the old faults survive in a different form. Rightly relieved of the danger of opposition obstruction, the Government has not bothered about parliamentary opinion. All too frequently it has shown no consideration whatever for the convenience of Members or the efficient working of Parliament.

Second, oral question day. Debré described it as the opposition's time, in which the Government's critics could freely debate questions on which they wished to attack the Ministers. The opposition has failed, and failed badly, to use the opportunities that question day could provide—though the senators have made much better use of it than the deputies. But the Government has not given them much encouragement, and a rather timid attempt to improve matters has been blocked by the Constitutional Council, taking once again an attitude even more Gaullist than the Government. The Government soon developed a bad practice of sending along a single Minister to answer all the questions down for debate on a given day. Clearly there can be no useful debate when the Minister's statement is simply a departmental brief read by a man with no knowledge of, responsibility for, or interest in the subject. The Assembly therefore adopted a proposal, made by a Gaullist Member, that Ministers should only be allowed to pass a question on to a colleague to answer if the house consented. But the Constitutional Council ruled that this was unconstitutional. The Assembly further wished to change question day from Friday, when most Members want to go to their constituencies, to a morning sitting mid-week, and to add an hour to the afternoon so as to keep the same total time; the Council ruled that they could change the day only by sacrificing the hour in the afternoon and so reducing the time for debate.

Those restrictions have made oral question day if not a laughingstock at best an occasion for raising trivial constituency grievances rather than real national issues. The opposition gets a reasonable share of the time, though not a preponderance, because the Presidents' Conference still, as in the Fourth Republic, divides it proportionately between the parties. This is not very serious, as most questions from opposition and majority alike are of purely local interest.

Oral question day was not as badly used in the second term as it was in the first. But it is certainly not an occasion when the opposition can dispose of the house's time to discuss whatever topic will, at that particular moment, most thoroughly embarrass the Government—for, after all, what is the purpose of an opposition except to draw public attention to the weaknesses and misdeeds of the Government and the grievances which its policies arouse? But oral question day cannot be such an opportunity for opposition time since it is, in the last resort, controlled by the majority. The Presidents' Conference decides which questions to call, in which category and in what order, and when it votes—which it does very rarely—the parties are mandated according to their numbers in the Assembly (as they have been since 1954). The Government's critics can therefore get their way only by persuading their political opponents, and it is hardly surprising that while their innocuous criticisms are debated frequently, a really awkward and controversial question rarely finds its way to the order paper at a moment when it might embarrass the Government. For example, when the first talks with the National Liberation Front [FLN] were held during the Algerian war in June 1960, the leader of the Algerian settler deputies tried to put down a question for debate; it was refused time by the Presidents' Conference. In May 1963, several opposition Members wanted to debate the winegrowers' grievances just before an important by-election in a wine-growing constituency; they were allowed plenty of time for debate but nearly all of it was arranged *after* the by-election was safely over. Similarly, in 1964, a debate on the Government's use of the official radio and television was allowed but given far less time than the opposition wanted. On the other hand, the Prime Minister took the first opportunity to debate an opposition question on his own role in the Government because he thought, rightly, that he could turn it to his own advantage. Responsibility for the failure of question day cannot rest exclusively with the ineptitude of opposition deputies unable to adapt to a new situation, for the majority has both the power and the will to block any attempt by the opposition to use its opportunity to criticize the Government in a damaging way. The majority can accept debate at times convenient to itself but can stifle criticism when the opposition might benefit. Surely it must bear some of the blame for Members' disillusionment.

My third example is the way in which legislation can be amended. As in the old days, bills still go first to committee for consideration, though it is the Government's draft which is debated on the floor. The committee, however, still puts its point of view in the floor debate. As in previous Republics, speaking time on the floor is allocated roughly equally between the four interested groups: the Government, the committee, the majority, and the opposition. But this arrangement has quite different results today from those it had in the past. Then the committee was expected to represent the views of those Members of the house who specialized in the subject discussed, and it spoke through a *rapporteur* who might well belong to an opposition party. Now the existence of a majority has changed everything. All committee chairmanships go to members of the majority, who also report all important bills. The four-sided arrangement of debating time therefore means that the majority enjoys three shares of it, speaking through Gaullist ministers, Gaullist *rapporteurs,* and Gaullist party spokesmen, while the fourth share has to be divided between all the opposition parties. It is true that this has no importance on nonpolitical bills and that the house can play a real part in shaping a measure like the reform of the adoption law which the Assembly amended and then adopted unanimously in 1966. It is also true that the opposition may not find itself short of time, that when it does the majority sometimes concedes some, and that Gaullist *rapporteurs* are often very critical of the Government and produce very vigorous debates. M. Poirier's report on the education budget in 1964 has since been quoted frequently by opposition leaders, and perhaps offers them some consolation for the fact that in the debate in which he spoke the opposition had 2 hours 10 minutes in all, Gaullist deputies had 7 hours, and André Malraux had 45 minutes to reply. The contrast to the House of Commons is marked: in the House the Speaker will always ensure that minority points of view are heard by giving them quite disproportionate time; if one wants a lively Parliament it seems a better arrangement. Once again, traditional arrangements that worked well enough in other circumstances have been carried over into a new Republic and a Parliament with a real majority. They have been retained precisely because they hampered the opposition and gave an advantage to the majority.

But this is only the first stage. The Government can, under Article 44, call for a package vote on the whole bill and any clauses or amendments it wishes to include. If a clause is unpopular or an amendment wins support among the majority, the Government can avoid a vote which might be difficult for it and can oblige its supporters either to keep the bill with the unpopular clause and without the popular amendment—or to lose the bill as a whole. The drastic procedure was invented by desperate

Fourth Republican Governments in the last decaying year of the old regime. In the first parliamentary term of the Fifth Republic, when there was no real majority and the Government had some justification for using all its resources, there were forty such package votes, an average of six a session. But in the second parliamentary term, where the Government had a loyal majority and should have been able to dispense with its clumsier weapons, there were 118 package votes in the corresponding period—an average of fifteen a session. The package vote was used both more frequently and more harshly as the Government's political difficulties diminished.

The package vote is useful to the Government because it saves majority Members from the embarrassment of having to vote openly against reasonable proposals which the Ministers are obstinately determined to resist. It is a small-scale variant of the vote of confidence procedure, which can allow the Government to carry a controversial bill for which there is no majority in either house provided only that fewer than half the deputies are willing at that moment to overthrow the Government and face a general election.

Even now we have not completed the description of the Government's advantages in legislative procedure. For the new mechanism for settling differences between the two houses is in practice really a means by which the Government can get its way against both of them—always provided, once again, that its followers are not prepared to throw it out. With the Senate normally in opposition, the Assembly now always, if the bill under discussion is at all controversial, sends to conference committees only representatives of the majority. On paper this should allow the majority to get its way. But in fact the system works differently. If a conference committee reaches agreement, its draft proposals come before the two houses only if the Government so chooses and only with such amendments as the Government accepts. In practice this means that the houses do not discuss the conference committee's report, but the Government's modification of that report instead.

THE SPIRIT OF GOVERNMENT-PARLIAMENT RELATIONS

The real trouble is not, of course, in the details of procedure. It is in the spirit in which they are applied. A Government with no reliable majority may need procedural defenses against obstruction, but if it is politically secure, it can afford to adopt or interpret procedural rules which give the opposition full freedom to deploy its case. Unfortunately the French Government neither does this in fact nor even pays lip service to it in theory. For example: the Constitution still allows Parliament, just as in the old days when the Government was so much weaker, to delegate for a limited period to the Government the right to legislate by decree on matters within what is now defined as Parliament's normal sphere. These decrees have to be laid before Parliament by a date settled in the enabling act, but there is nothing to oblige the Government to allow them to be debated. In 1960 Parliament gave delegated powers to the Government to act against alcoholism, an acute problem which the deputies had never mustered the political courage to tackle themselves in the Third, Fourth, or Fifth Republics. The Government passed a number of decrees which its critics wished to challenge—and I hasten to add that on the substance of the question my sympathies are wholly with the Government. The Ministers never allowed a debate in Government time, and their majority blocked a debate at any other time. The Socialist party introduced a constitutional amendment bill requiring decrees passed under these conditions to lapse unless they were debated within six months, but the Government would not allow it to be debated. After four years a Socialist spokesman protested, but the reply from the Minister of Justice was: "You want the minority to decide the parliamentary timetable. No democracy in the world allows that." I wonder how many Gaullists would have continued to hold this conception of democracy if M. Mitterand had won the presidential election in 1965 and used the same procedures against them.

The same right to legislate by decree was invoked in 1967 when the electorate had returned only a tiny Gaullist majority. Both the Government's moderate supporters and its moderate critics expected their views to receive more attention than hitherto from the executive. Instead the ministers required their unhappy followers to vote a delegation of power removing from all parliamentary scrutiny a major measure reorganizing the social services. It was this kind of unwillingness to listen which provoked the public exasperation that was to find such a dramatic outlet in May 1968, and—less dramatically but more decisively —eroded de Gaulle's support and led to his defeat in April 1969.

I am afraid these remarks seem rather like a Fourth Republican polemic against the Fifth. Let me therefore repeat that I think most (not all) of the reforms of 1958 were improvements. But experience does seem to me to confirm—not surprisingly— that a Government armed against all imaginable dangers enjoys a position of excessive strength which it is likely to abuse. The constitution makers of the Fifth Republic assumed that it was utopian to hope for a disciplined parliamentary majority and therefore relied on formal rules to achieve the results which are attained in Britain through party discipline. They drew the new rules from many different sources: the strictly Gaullist proposals for a strong President able to call for a referendum, the traditional conservative solution of giving the Government the right to dissolve the Assembly at will, the procedural changes which had been worked out in successive Parliaments over the previous thirty years, and the peculiar gimmicks (such as the vote of censure and package vote rules) invented by desperate Governments in the decadent period of the Fourth Republic. Having assembled all these weapons in their arsenal, the Gaullists then found themselves with a loyal majority after all. The opposition failed to adapt to this new situation and did not use the opportunities they still had. The Government failed to adapt because it used its overwhelming procedural advantages to restrict the opposition's opportunities, even when the political situation would have allowed it safely to give its critics a free rein.

You can have a legislature like the Congress of the United States, which cannot overturn the Government and which takes for granted that its duty is to arrive at a point of view of its own on the bills and policies which the Government puts forward. You can have a legislature like the British House of Commons, to which the Government is responsible and which takes it for granted that the Government can get its way in the end but subject to the full freedom of the Members to persuade the Government to change its mind or the people to repudiate the Government later. France did not have either before and she does not have either now. In the old regime Parliament dominated the Government and denied itself effective leadership. In the new regime the Government dominates Parliament and denies itself effective criticism. It is quite true that the Assembly can still, in theory and in practice, throw out the Government if a clear majority of Members can be found to do so. But this does not make it an effective Parliament, and if this were the only way a British opposition could make its criticism felt, the House of Commons would be in poor shape. These developments are not at all surprising. All Governments have a natural tendency to believe that opposition and criticism are quite right in principle but that they become demagogic and irresponsible when directed at Ministers so reasonable, so well-intentioned, so enlightened and patriotic as themselves. That is why they can never be trusted with wholly unchecked power.

6

Parliament and Nation-Building: England and India

HENRY C. HART

The role of parliament in the new nations created since World War II is bound to differ from the role of this institution in the older states of Europe and North America. It is remarkable that parliaments, which are the products of European political experience, have been so widely established in Asia and Africa. In the selection below, Henry C. Hart, a long-time student of Indian politics, explains that the role of parliament in new states can only be compared to the role the institution played at a comparable stage of European political history. By comparing the Indian parliament today with the British House of Commons in the eighteenth century, he identifies the function of parliament in nation-building and reminds us that conflicting expectations of parliament arise not only from cross-national differences but from cross-temporal differences as well.

The third Indian Parliament to complete a full five-year term since Indian independence accomplished many of the things typical of representative legislatures everywhere. It passed 273 bills,

This chapter is a condensation of a paper originally presented at the Sixty-fifth Annual Meeting of the American Political Science Association, September 1969. It is reprinted here by permission of the author.

including legislation on major and controversial subjects such as restricting the use of gold for ornaments (an antismuggling measure), regulating factory bonuses, protecting the working conditions of the poor laborers who roll indigenous cigarettes, determining the language in which government would communicate, and collecting compulsory savings to help pay for the defense build-up after the Chinese attack. It gave Members an opportunity to check up on literally thousands of matters of government administration by means of questions put to ministers —twenty-five per day, on the average—and on broad policy by means of brief, free-wheeling debates on major matters Members felt had gone wrong, sometimes linked to motions of censure. These last, of course, were defeated by the governing Congress Party's disciplined majority, 360 out of 493 elected members, but they made headlines for the tiny percentage of the Indian population reached by the press.

This being so, it was striking that the Indian Parliament was charged officially with quite a different additional task. Prime Minister Nehru used these words in opening the newly elected popular House of Parliament in 1962: "India is a country of manifold variety. . . . It has people who differ in their religions and their customs and there are people who are called minorities and the like. This House has a great task, if I may use the word, of molding them into a single entity, that is India, that is the people of India."[1] On that occasion the President, Radhakrishnan, was less eloquent but more explicit, referring to the "task of nation-building for which the Parliament has both the continuing and ultimate responsibility. . . ."[2]

India certainly requires nation-building. The severity of the problem is roughly equivalent to that of making one nation of all Western and Central Europe. Population and area are comparable. The number of major languages is greater in Europe (20) than India (14), but India has the more diverse linguistic structure and far more speakers of preliterate tribal languages. India has as many kinds of Hindus as Europe has Christians, but in addition it has an 11 percent Muslim minority, something as hard to integrate as European Islam might have been in the immediate wake of the Ottoman Empire.

The Indian legacy includes only two major entries on the asset side of the comparative ledger. One is the enlistment of some millions of Indians, including an unknown number of the village population, in the anticolonial struggle under Gandhi. The most evident fruit of that experience is the nationwide Congress Party, still in control of the national government and, in 1962, of all but one state. Second is the complex of British-Indian institutions grown in place for well over a century: courts, law and other professions, independent press, city self-government, business corporations, trade unions, English-language colleges, a fine elite civil service, national and state legislatures. It was understandable that, as cracks appeared in the fabric of national unity, the leaders who had earned their high places in both institutional frameworks, revolutionary and colonial, should look to the meeting place of the two, the elected Parliament dominated by the Congress Party, to meet the challenge to unity.

But Parliament had been transplanted from Westminster to Delhi to enact laws, to oversee administration, and later to evoke public opinion and air grievances. It had not been intended to integrate the nation. Nehru and Radhakrishnan may have been calling for the impossible. But their challenge to Parliament was also a challenge to political science. India has the best-rooted parliamentary institutions among the excolonial nations. India's nation-building problem is the most severe. Is the expectation that the former can supply a solution to the latter a giant leap into the unknown? Or can political science make some predictions about the capacity of parliament to perform nation-building functions?

COMPARISON IN TIME

One way to look for an answer is to study the experience of some elected legislature which operated continuously right through the phases and crises of nation-building so we can observe the result. The obvious candidate for study is the British Parliament, for it is the one on which the Indian was modeled and has been uniquely well recorded.

In order to make a valid comparison in time, we need a theory which can conceive of present Indian developments of national unity-disunity as well as of historic British developments as stages and variations of a single set of processes. We need measures by which we can determine at what point in the British past we should look for possible contributions of the Westminster Parliament to these processes. Fortunately, as to the basic processes of nation-building, Karl Deutsch has supplied the theory we require.[3] In his original (it would be fair to say now-classical) formulation of this theory, Deutsch saw a double trend. Under certain conditions of the last five centuries, human interdependence has increased with urbanization, a market economy, and industrialization. Interdependent people are drawn into intense communication with one another and with leading groups and urban centers. This is *social mobilization,* both a precondition and, in its later stages, a product of nation formation. If the underlying culture of the mobilized has been one, they tend to undergo simultaneous *cultural assimilation,* becoming conscious of themselves as a nationality. If their cultures were diverse (e.g., if they were illiterate in different languages) they may undergo *cultural differentiation,* also induced by social mobilization.

Deutsch, Cutright, and others have also suggested statistical indicators of social mobilization. The two most reliable are urbanization and the growth of nonagricultural employment and income. The end result of a good deal of demographic exploration and comparison is that the period in Britain's social mobilization most comparable to India's current status is the second quarter of the eighteenth century. At that time something like 15 percent of the population of England and Wales lived in towns and cities of above 5,000 population, compared to 18 percent in modern India. The population dependent on agriculture made up 50 to 60 percent of the whole as against 70 percent in India today; 40–45 percent of English income came from agriculture as against about 45 percent in India. The means of cultural assimilation (deferring for a moment the question of language) are harder to compare. England and Wales had already (though here we extrapolate from a shaky statistic) a higher percent of literates, taking men and women together. They certainly did not have so high a proportion of school-age children in school.

But we cannot reconcile all differences in social mobilization along the time dimension. The contrast in size remains. In 1690 Gregory King used the hearth-tax returns to prepare the first trustworthy estimate of the population of England and Wales. The total as revised by modern demographers was 4.8 million, a little over 1 percent of the 1961 Indian population. There are only a few states within India as small as England and Wales were then.

London was *the* city of England and Wales during the eighteenth century. With 422,000 people in 1690, it was more than ten times the size of any other town, and it had much over half of all urban population. India is a multimetropolis country with cities over one million strong in most of its major language states.

One could continue to find differences in the social contexts. But they would all be there to weaken a comparison of England 1961 to India 1961. What we have done is to highlight the remaining differences by minimizing those associated with stages of social mobilization. If one wishes to compare England's experience with a parliament to India's, there is no better analogue to Nehru's India than Robert Walpole's early eighteenth-century England. Did Parliament then exhibit any integrative functions? If so, under what conditions did they show results?

First Function: Regulating Succession

England had been defined overtly by Henry VIII in 1533 as against the Church of Rome. The threat of a Catholic king was a double threat to that nationality. Internationally, it could involve

England in the defense of Catholic countries. Domestically, as the Exclusion Bill of 1680 declared, upon succession of a Catholic monarch "nothing is more manifest than that a total change of religion within these kingdoms would ensue." To us the reasoning is unpersuasive, but the concern for the identity of the nation is transparent. The ban on succession of a Catholic was repeated in 1689, 1701, and 1707. Parliament involved itself further with the regulation of the monarch's conduct. He might not go out of England, Scotland, or Ireland without the consent of Parliament. Parliament must be convened or if in session, continued, upon the death of a monarch. Regulating the succession was an episodic task. The significant points for us are that the nation had, at this stage of development, to define itself in the person of its king and that it was Parliament that accomplished the task.

Second Function: Unification of Nationalities

England is often held as the model of early and thoroughgoing achievement of territorial nationality. In the middle of the eighteenth century the nationality of four of every ten inhabitants of the British Isles was in conflict.[4] Parliament was not the only arena of that conflict, but it was an essential one.

For our purposes the cases of Wales and Scotland provide instructive comparisons. Wales, most vulnerable, was conquered by the English before a Welsh regnum of parliament could be instituted. Rule by English kings of the Welsh Tudor line was accepted with pride.[5] Henry VIII, second of that line, drew 24 Welsh members into Parliament and consolidated his administrative control of Wales on the English pattern. The act of union (1536) coincided with his break with Rome. Wales came through the Reformation with the Church of England as its church. Only at the turn of the nineteenth century did evangelism lay a new basis for Welsh nationality;[6] by that time the industrial revolution was cutting a new cleavage through the urbanizing society of England and Wales. Meanwhile, in the eighteenth century the 24 Welsh members of Parliament were quiet, unconcerned with larger issues, whether of Britain or of Wales.[7] The fact that the majority of the people spoke Welsh remained a recessive characteristic; in Deutsch's terms the linguistically Welsh remained an unmobilized majority.

In Scotland we can see the semiautomatic processes of social mobilization and cultural assimilation (as Deutsch called them) working sometimes in different directions from the conscious institution-building processes. As to language and status of social mobilization, there were two Scotlands. The Lowlands had by 1700 anglicized their speech;[8] the Highlands still used Gaelic. The Lowlands had by 1700 a mercantile economy, the Highlands grazed sheep and grew oats and barley via a tribal social organization. In the sixteenth and seventeenth centuries two experiences drew both sections into relationship with England. The Scottish Reformation was even more anti-Papist than England's, and subsequent involvement of ministers of the Scottish kirk in the religious controversies of England cut across the Scotch-English cleavage. Installation of a Scottish king (James I) upon the throne of England furthered unification as in the earlier Welsh case.

But tension was growing in 1700 in both politics and trade. The Scottish parliament in Edinburgh was attracting esteem and acting with a certain amount of independence. Merchants in the Lowland cities, hitherto the pro-English element, were chafing at their exclusion by law from the English market. They tried through the Darien Company to break into trade with North America; they blamed English undercutting for the resulting bankruptcy.

The threat which moved the English merchant aristocracy in Parliament to concede trade rights to the Scots was a threat to orderly succession. The parliament in Edinburgh refused to acknowledge Anne as successor to William. A bargaining situation was thus set up in which the English ruling element could gain stability by conceding the conditions of prosperity to their Scottish counterparts. The Act of Union of 1707 demonstrates the balance of interests.[9] It stipulates first the conditions of the customs union and of trading rights overseas, distributes taxation, assumes the debts of the Darien failure, and recognizes the separate churches established in the two countries. Upon this bargain the Edinburgh parliament dissolved itself, naming 45 members to the House of Commons and 16 peers to the Lords. Now the unification of the nationalities was cast into the single arena of Parliament.

THIRD FUNCTION: CONSOLIDATION OF A NATIONAL ELITE

J. H. Plumb has studied the eighteenth century with the researches of the economic and social historians in focus. Plumb concerned himself with the question we address: "How societies come to accept a pattern of political authority and the institutions that are required for its translation into government." He found his answers to that question in the experience of half of the century and he sums them up thus: "In England . . . there were three major factors: single party government; the legislature firmly under executive control; and a sense of common identity in those who wielded economic, social, and political power."[10]

Let us examine, in reverse order, these explanations for the legitimization of a system of rule in a nation firmly founded but yet to undergo its great socioeconomic transformation. "Those who wielded economic, social, and political power" are characterized by Plumb as "men of property, particularly those of high social standing, whether aristocrats or linked to the aristocracy, whose tap-root was in land, but whose side-roots reached out to commerce, industry, and finance."[11] Parliament was, for these men, a necessary means of profiting. Most eighteenth-century bills were, in the modern sense, private bills. Parliament enclosed their fields, chartered their toll roads, toward mid-century authorized their spurt of canal building.[12] On a vast scale, and in many indirect ways, including defense, it made the world safe for their chartered trading monopolies of which the East India Company was giant.

Second, this "natural elite" governed through institutions whose control was, in the early eighteenth century, fused into what in modern parlance would be a "power structure." Separate institutions were in place from medieval times: king and court, Lords, Commons, borough councils, and shire officers, the lawyers and judges. But what happened in the early years of the eighteenth century was a penetration of those boundaries to facilitate control of the whole by a small group of the natural elite overlapping in their membership year after year. The monarch was part of this group, the strongest figure. But he was not independent of it for, unlike the Tudors who ruled on the proceeds of church lands, he had to have appropriations from taxes, and wars were frequent. Plumb shows the growth of the executive services from 1700 to 1714, particularly of the navy, of a standing army, and of the Treasury with its nationwide tax collecting apparatus.[13] The king was at the head of this swollen executive. But for running it he was doubly dependent. He needed more knowledgeable administrative ability than his personal court could provide (as George I's German aides demonstrated) and he needed leadership of the Commons and the Lords. He needed what the natural elite power structure could provide. And so "after 1694 the Whig aristocracy was concerned not to limit but strengthen monarchy and authority."[14]

The great block to fusion of governing power in the hands of the king and his elite ministers was the independence of Parliament. Plumb puts it bluntly: "The key to political instability was Parliament, a medieval institution launched by the Tudors into a world for which it was unfitted."[15] Contrary to our general image of oligarchy, Parliament emerged from the Revolution of 1689 based upon a considerable electorate. Inflation had lowered the significance of the 40 shilling freehold. Plumb thinks there were 200,000 voters. That is two-fifths of the heads of families Gregory King counted as self-supporting. It is one-sixth of adult males, compared to one-half of adult males voting in an Indian election. Moreover, at the turn of the century English voters were going to the polls much more often: a general election every two years, on the average, between 1700 and 1715;[16] in our Indian analogue the interval is five years.

> An electorate, therefore, for the first time in English history, had come into being. This new political nation proved very mettlesome, very contrary, very fickle in its moods; above all it helped to give substance to the parties and give them added power. . . . Until this electorate was reduced, subjected, or prevented from voting, there was no hope whatsoever that England would achieve political stability.[17]

The new "political nation" was harnessed in two ways. Before 1689 borough charters were "remodeled" by Charles II and James II, often restricting the vote to borough councils only. After the Revolution, town property owners claimed the franchise, and many elections were disputed. Porritt finds that 127 of the 218 English and Welsh boroughs had had such disputes determined by 1729.[18] Determination was by Parliament and "Whig Parliaments decided time and time again in favor of a narrow franchise."[19] In 1729 Parliament froze the electorate in all those 127 cases against further appeals. So the electorate actually shrank. But the main device for control was official patronage. Candidates were more and more dependent upon it as election expenses mounted. It was in the Robert Walpole ministry, 1721 to 1742, that patronage was raised to the system which prevented any election from overturning a Government. "Now was finally elaborated that admixture of royal and ministerial influence which one Government after another employed for the next hundred years; the exploiting of patronage in Britain, Ireland, and the Indies, of local magistracy, military command, bribes to members and constituencies, press subsidies, peerages, and pensions."[20]

In short, the separate institutions of a balanced constitution were fused—legislative, executive, and local—for single control. And in 1715 parties were fused as well. The Tories were foolishly implicated in a military action in the Highlands designed to restore the Stuart Pretender. Walpole never let King George forget Tory treachery; the Whigs passed an act extending the life of Parliaments from three to seven years, and the Whig oligarchy was in place. To be sure, a triumphant party is not *ipso facto* a consolidated national elite. But the Whigs had, since 1689, lost their zeal for dissent; they intended to rule with the king, not against him, and they certainly failed Burke's test of being "united upon some particular principle." There was no longer, by 1721, any Whig ideology. That was partly because the rationale of the Whig tradition, as John Locke had stated it, was common currency among all ambitious Members of Parliament.[21] It was still more because the "most powerful groups in the Whig party became preoccupied with the processes rather than the principles of government. They wanted to capture the Government machine and run it."[22]

Was the "Whig ascendancy" (by Walpole's time we could more accurately call it ex-Whig) a party? We are in a position now to give a modern answer to this modern historians' controversy: Not if party means an institution autonomous of government, not if it means constituency associations. The Whig oligarchs were aristocrats with economic, usually social, and local political power bases of their own, and those propertied bases were part of the modernizing trading and manufacturing economy. But as to the political system they controlled, it was as much single-party, and as much executive machine, as the "party-states" Zolberg[23] sees in West Africa today, or the machine of the American city boss fifty years ago. It was a fused system run by a national elite.

Fourth Function: Linkage

Plumb asks a question strikingly relevant to the modern interpretation of Indian politics:

> Were there then two worlds of politics in the eighteenth century
> —a tight political establishment, linked to small groups of power-
> ful political managers in the provinces, who controlled Parliament,
> the executive, and all that was effective in the nation, and outside
> this an amorphous mass of political sentiment that found ex-
> pression in occasional hysteria and impotent polemic, but whose
> effective voice in the nation was negligible?[24]

Plumb sees the oligarchy stabilizing its power in the first half of
the century. He sees also the "political nation" gaining numbers
and vigor: political pamphlets, papers, petitions, meetings, plays,
indeed political issues and agitations, grew right through the century. Plumb has a remarkable phrase: "the public grew as the
electorate diminished."[25] The key to understanding is two
worlds variably linked, and we can distinguish three variables.

First, some constituencies were remotely linked, others directly. Most remote were the Welsh and Scotch counties and
boroughs. Except on issues concerning their own areas, these
Members, 24 from Wales and 45 from Scotland, voted like
sheep for the Government. The Scotch situation was, however,
peculiar, for Scotland was a nationality very much to be integrated in the eighteenth-century Parliament. It was integrated
through patronage.

Robert Walpole organized this political industry. For him the
Duke of Argyle, later Henry Dundas, delivered the 45 Scottish
MPs to vote like sheep for the ministry in power. In return more
than their share of places in the overseas services went to Scottish graduates. It was an indirect and asymmetrical linkage, but it
drew the young men who would otherwise have been Scottish na-
tionalists into an expanding British political elite.

At the other extreme was London: organized, alert, diverse,
near, and potentially threatening. Walpole tried controlling London politics as other boroughs had been controlled, by remodeling its charter and restricting more power to the aldermen. He
could get the support of bankers, but not of the merchants, great
or small, nor of the craftsmen and journeymen. "In his handling
of London, unlike Scotland . . . Walpole secured not even a
momentary success. . . ."[26]

In between were the active and inactive counties, the vestigial boroughs and the rising trading cities. How could the active constituencies, often underrepresented, make their needs felt? One way grew out of the much keener contests of their elections. When finally in 1768 a London suburban electorate returned the outlawed but unrestrained militant Wilkes, the resulting conflict radicalized British politics for years.[27]

The second variable is faction within the Parliament. While faction was at the oligarchy level it had no linkage value. As issues emerged, factions were able to rally support through elections, and the way to parties in the modern sense was open.

Issues, then, constitute the third variable. "Issues," Plumb says, "abounded."[28] But their potential for creating lines of influence between constituents and Members varied widely. The measures capable of arousing a public were, it seems from the eighteenth-century cases, of two general sorts. First, there were those that put the government into the relatively isolated householder's life in a dramatic way. The malt tax in Scotland, the cider tax of the 1760s to the country gentlemen—these were such measures. Most dramatic was Walpole's Excise Bill of 1733, a seemingly innocuous measure to replace customs duty on tobacco with an inland tax. But agitation by pamphlets and London mobs, coupled with a threat to Walpole's parliamentary majority and a split in his party, forced him to withdraw the bill. The other kind of measure, even more explosive, is illustrated by the mild act of 1753 permitting Parliament to naturalize fully the few Jews who had already gained some rights. It was an issue threatening to nationality, of the same general category as Spanish atrocities to British seamen, and the public clamor forced a surprised Parliament to repeal the "Jew Bill" in the same year.[29]

FIFTH FUNCTION: INCUBATING AN OPPOSITION

Joseph LaPalombara and Myron Weiner suggest as a result of their worldwide comparisons of parties as agencies of development that: "competitive-party systems seem to materialize naturally and logically in societies where the pressure to create party organizations was initially felt in the legislature."[30] Lipset and Rokkan, comparing European parties as to their bases in social cleavage, make the significant assumption that party-forming cleavages occur in response to what they call "a central core of cooperating 'nation-builders' controlling major elements of the machinery of the 'state.' "[31] We have observed conditions developing in England whereby a nation-building elite was consolidated, consolidated in Parliament. But this occurred early in the century, by about 1727. What were the remaining conditions sufficient for lasting party cleavage to emerge? One obvious condition was the strengthening, extension, and proliferation of linkages between the elite and the "political nation." Lipset and Rokkan discuss such linkages in terms of thresholds of access and influence to national decisions. This would support the contention that parties were impossible before the Reform Bill of 1832. We might also discuss it in terms of channels of communication between Parliament and constituencies, channels which opened with newspaper reporting of Parliament in the period 1768 to 1774.[32]

As one reads Sir Lewis Namier's great studies of the House of Commons in the last half of the eighteenth century, another factor comes prominently into view. Government acquired, in those years, a vast new burden of responsibility. This was not enclosures and turnpikes, but public in the modern sense. Nor was it defense of England, which would not have divided the country. As in the excise crisis, "a powerful wave of feeling swept the country," but the Government could not withdraw the issue. Namier sees it building up: it did not impinge on the voters in the general election of 1768, it was mentioned in ten constituencies in 1774, by 1780 it had formed political parties and brought down the Government.[33] That issue was the American war. Lord North's ministry and the king stood steadfast on that issue during twelve years. The Rockingham Whigs, equally steadfast on the opposite side, were aristocrats. Upon that issue they had in self-defense to try to raise a public following. In this sense our evidence upholds the LaPalombara-Weiner view that parties were incubated in Parliament, but requires also the Lipset-Rokkan explanation that they arose in reaction to a nation-building elite, vigorously wielding the machinery of state. English parliamentary factions changed to parties when Government began doing something major, continuing, controversial, and salient to the voters.

PARLIAMENT AND NATION-BUILDING IN INDIA

The most relevant of the British experiences we can now distill into propositions, pointing to the functions of the Indian Parliament in nation-building and perhaps to some of their conditions of success. We cannot yet state these as hypotheses or find data capable of testing them, though we can illustrate how such testing might be done.

Parliament and Succession

Until the definition of a nation is embodied in its institutions, and a national leadership established, succession to the positions of chief executive will threaten that definition. Parliament will regulate succession to control that threat.

The function of choosing a prime minister, now regarded as latent in the British House of Commons,[34] has indeed been a crucial, though infrequent, function of the majority party in Parliament in India. We have a good account of that process extending through the replacement of Nehru and of Shastri.[35] Michael Brecher shows that it was not the majority party in Parliament alone that made the succession decision; the national organization of the party and its state chiefs had a prior say. But it is interesting to note that each of the factions which formed in the struggle for Nehru's succession was convened by an MP (in one case a former Member). And it was the alignment of MPs that enabled specific numerical forecasts to be prepared of the outcome.

To what extent were considerations of national integration salient to the decision? Selig Harrison forecast at the start of the 1960s that language divisions would become the immediate threat to Indian unity.[36] The succession struggle assumed the form of a contest between a candidate who would use government authority to extend the use of Hindi to non-Hindi states (Morarji Desai) and another (Lal Bahadur Shastri) who, though representing a Hindi state in Parliament, would go slow in extending its mandatory use. Shastri was chosen under the leadership of a non-Hindi coalition.

Charisma is still an important, perhaps a necessary, attribute of an Indian Prime Minister.[37] To many millions of voters, his personality—dress, speech, daily habits, ceremonial observances, style of public appearance—provides the strongest and probably the only current symbol of the nation. It is the fidelity of that symbol to the definition upon which the nation was founded that is at stake. It is a great strength of the Indian constitution that it provides a plural representative body which can, in an official and dignified process, settle that struggle.

Leader-Voter Linkage

At the stage of consolidating a national leadership, that leadership develops latent linkage with nonvoters of the national culture, indirect linkage with constituencies of differing culture.

India has generated regional, language-culture elites especially in Bengal, Madras, and Maharashtra.[38] At the national level it developed an intelligentsia, communicating and transmitting its norms in the English language. In terms of the culture gap between national leadership and local or regional leaderships, all India repeats the relationship of England to Scotland. The analogy holds in two respects. First, the all-India intelligentsia shares with the principal regions of India the legitimizing experience of a long and demanding struggle in the name of national ideals. Second, no present part of India was defined out of the nation as Catholic Ireland was. But in other crucial respects there is contrast. There is no dominant Indian culture corresponding to English culture in Britain; the national leadership is, in any event, acculturated in English. Institutions of rule are not fused into a single power pyramid but remain autonomous save at the level of charismatic leadership, e.g., by Nehru. And there are the further modern linkages of parties and elections which we will presently examine. It is surprising, therefore, to turn up, in the recent history of parliamentary decision-making in India, a series of cases in which a wholly unanticipated public reaction to newly established law or policy, expressed outside the formal processes of representation, results in a reversal of government decision. One such case is strikingly parallel to the Excise Bill of 1733.

The Chinese attack of 1962 meant to Nehru's ministry a more than doubled defense budget. It also demonstrated a wholly unanticipated outpouring of popular support for the war effort, measured both by voluntary donations (e.g., peasant women's silver anklets) to the National Defense Fund and by enlistment rates. The Finance Minister announced in his 1963 budget a balanced array of new taxes. One, Compulsory Deposits, had far more political significance than the others. It would have drawn into forced saving of a modest percent of income about half the Indian population: most textile mill workers, middle-ranking government clerks, shopkeepers, and perhaps half of all owner-cultivators of farms. The novelty of the outreach becomes clearer if we compare the 60 million families to be affected with the one and one-half million already paying personal or corporate income tax.

Parliament debated Compulsory Deposits vigorously, and the Finance Minister explained it on the national radio. The bill was amended and in three months passed. India's post offices began to prepare to collect compulsory savings; deductions were, of course, taken first from national government employees.

The aftermath of war brought inflation. People on fixed incomes suffered. By the summer of 1963, the previous October's outpouring of patriotism had evaporated. The Communist Party attacked Compulsory Deposits via agitation in many towns and all mill centers where they had cadre. They brought to Delhi a petition of protest said to contain 10 to 12 million names. A giant procession, recruited from many cities, carried the petition to Parliament. Nehru accepted the resignation of the Finance Minister who had introduced the scheme. The new minister immediately suspended forced savings without benefit of parliamentary repeal.

Note that, in this case, the burden to be imposed was real and great, relative either to past burdens or ability to pay. But in this case all classes of men and women on whom the burden would fall had the vote. Yet public outcry came three months after parliamentary decision, and only when collections had started. We can, in this case, learn a little more about the obstructions to feedback. I asked the 189 MPs I interviewed in the year following the Compulsory Deposits episode whether in their visits to their constituencies they had either received reactions from constituents to the plan or told constituents their own position on it. Replies came from 159. Almost all (138) heard *something* from constituents before or after passage of the bill. Two-thirds (104) gave some indication of their own position. These figures are not very remarkable since the test of communication is such a weak one. But there is a narrower finding of significance. Half the reactions reported by MPs came solely from "middle classes" (meaning in Indian terminology the top 1 or 2 percent of the income brackets), salaried persons, government employees, or urban-educated people. An equal number of MPs (69 in each case) had feedback from the four-fifths (on the average) of their constituents who are peasants or trade unionists, about half of whom would be reached by the measure. The largest single group of protesters, and the only group reported to have protested before enactment (and thus to be parallel to the British Excise Bill public) were stationmasters and other railway officers.

During the stage of legislative decision, then, we see public reaction to bills, even of a kind which reach into the family economy of large fractions of the populace, as latent. Ministers accustomed to thinking of Parliament as a reflection of national opinion are taken aback by the virulence of public reaction to the execution of such measures. Such a public reaction is episodic, even when organized by political parties.

Parties as Links

Parties, trying to gain power by votes, tighten leader-voter linkage in two specific ways: communication and recruitment to leadership.

There is no reason, a priori, for a new nation to repeat all the painful troubles of the pioneers. India has borrowed a piece of social technology, the political party, from the England of the nineteenth and twentieth century. May it not shortcut the developmental steps of the eighteenth century?

Again our Indian data can illustrate the meaning which comparison gives, but it cannot put the hypothesis to the test. Among 189 Members of Parliament interviewed, 108 made up a 30 percent random sample of 360 Congress Party members. Eighty were of the large number of opposition parties and independents: 60 percent of the aggregate opposition, but not a random sample, tending slightly to overweight the oppositionists active in the affairs of the House. Each interviewee was told: "I want to find out how well your party serves to connect you to the individual voters in your constituency." It is a tall order. The Indian parliamentary constituency averages almost 900,000 inhabitants, difficult of access and not often organized either in towns or associations of any kind.

The more than one-third of constituencies in which Members claimed that party organizations reached at least half of all villages or town wards is a very generous estimate. What is interesting is the difference Table 1 shows between the Congress Party and the aggregate opposition situation. There is no difference in party linkage when the MP is himself passive as to organizational work in the constituency party. But when he engages himself in party building, his efforts are more productive in the Con-

TABLE 1: *Party as Connecting Link between MP and Voters in Constituency: Interviewees of Congress and Combined Opposition Parties*

	MP Role Passive		MP Role Active		Total	
	Congress N = 74	Opposition N = 35	Congress N = 34	Opposition N = 45	Congress N = 108	Opposition N = 80
Party fails to reach half of villages or wards	76%	77%	38%	·56%	64%	65%
Party reaches more than half of villages or wards	24%	23%	62%	44%	36%	35%
TOTALS	100%	100%	100%	100%	100%	100%

gress, the prestigious and then-dominant party. We have the hint that the nation-building party is a great resource but does not, two decades after the independence struggle, possess self-sustaining energy.

Now read Table 1 horizontally. Over one-third of Congressmen, but over half of oppositionists, busy themselves with party work in the constituency.[39] The party system taken as a whole induces organizational activity on the part of the Member. But it induces it in building opposition parties, some regional, some national, some of questionable commitment to the constituted order. The contrast would be sharpened dramatically if we segregated from the opposition the 15 nonparty members.

We can explore another role of party as link—that of recruiter. The strategic constituencies are the rural ones (defined as having less than 20 percent urban population). For in the towns there are other avenues for the ambitious man or woman to make his entry into politics: trade unions and trade associations, boards of secondary schools, cultural associations, agitations. But, especially in 1963, before new institutions of rural local government had operated extensively, it was a great leap from traditional village office, or semiprofessional position in a country town, to state or national candidacy.

In making the leap, college education is a great advantage. It inducts one into the English language and thus into the anglicized culture of which Parliament is part. Whether it is an advantage in maintaining close ties with rural constituents, however, is another matter. Table 2 shows that from rural constituencies the Congress Party was nominating the English-language-educated college graduates more frequently than were other parties. But that is not all. In the Congress, the non-English-educated MP may nurse his constituency, but he does not debate, serve on committees, or raise questions in the House. But half of the noncollege oppositionists were able to do so. There is good reason. The small opposition parties help MPs prepare questions to put on the floor, vie for debating time for hesitant Members, and parcel out responsibilities to make their criticisms heard.

TABLE 2: *Education and Participation in the Affairs of Parliament: MPs from Rural Constituencies, Congress and Opposition Interviewees*

	Congress Party		All Opposition and Independents	
	Participant N = 16	*Nonparticipant* N = 29	*Participant* N = 18	*Nonparticipant* N = 20
College-educated MPs	93%	38%	50%	25%
Less than college educated	7%	62%	50%	75%
TOTALS	100%	100%	100%	100%

Parties appeared in Great Britain at the end of the eighteenth century to exploit dissent generated by vigorous government programs. The programs were vigorous because they were conducted by a national elite in power which kept its base of support through patronage and through a good deal of responsiveness to the demands of a large sector of the active nation. The dissent supported an opposition because it organized new socially and economically influential groups both in the industrial cities and in the commercially active counties like Yorkshire.

On the Indian scene opposition parties are organizing dissent. They are using the modern techniques of party and the opportunities provided by fair elections conducted upon adult suffrage. What is missing from the scene is a government strengthening its own roots; evidently party organization is not accomplishing that any more than patronage is.

Representation: Virtual, Influential, Cooptative

An agrarian society becoming a nation within parliamentary norms affords three types of representation: virtual, influential, and cooptative. An active government facing party competition requires increasing support from influential representation.

Parties link Indian parliamentary policy-makers to voters only at the opposition fringes; competition has not tightened the great central links of the Congress. Neither mass communications nor interest associations of various sorts supply feedback to policy-makers or bring the needs of voters before them in forceful and policy-specific form. But fair elections conducted with adult franchise do put a very large number of men and women into roles of anticipating, articulating, and striving with whatever ingenuity and leverage they possess to get relief for the grievances of the people. We can conceive parliamentary democracy as a great free enterprise market, rewarding those who can make links effective. Does the Indian system work this way?

My information suggests rather strongly that it does. The distance measured by the reach of organization or by cultural norms, between the national decision-making arena in Delhi and the subcontinental mosaic of Indian constituencies, is enormous, beyond even the distance between London and the Scottish Highlands. Yet I found one MP in every four participating vigorously in both "worlds." My tests were composite ones. I ascertained the number and vigor of a Member's contacts and organized relations in his constituency. For his participation in Parliament I used as indices debating, asking questions, serving on committees, and also the informal activities of buttonholing ministers and exerting leadership in the parliamentary party. Most Members who were active in Parliament sacrificed constituency relations (ministers are the extreme, here) and vice versa. But 47 of the 189 managed to keep the connection between Parliament and constituency in their personal efforts. We might think of them as link members.

Curiously, however, MPs of traditionally learned castes (Brahmins and a few others) accomplished linkage in quite a different way from those of traditional ruling and estate-managing castes. To simplify, the former debated while the latter organized their constituencies and sought government works for them. Among this group of MPs who have found modern uses for traditional roles, some remain active in both "worlds" without conveying specific influence upon decisions in either direction. Picking up a traditional English term, we might call theirs *virtual* representation. They are the counterparts to Namier's country gentlemen who wanted to be in Parliament but not in the harness of ministries. Others wield specific political power thereby. I think of the deputy minister of a major ministry who maintained daily contact with his commercial farming constituency (in which he came from a dominant landed caste) by long-distance telephone calls discussing the marketing of the major commercial crop. Such men (they are a minority of the Congress link members) and the Marxist mobilizing intelligentsia from urban-industrial constituencies we might think of as providing *influential* representation.

India has almost no national patronage. It has, however, a kind of representation we might place in comparison with the 45 Scottish representatives of the eighteenth century. These are the holders of "reserved seats" to which only former untouchables (untouchability now being illegal as far as Indian law can reach) and members of tribal societies can be nominated. No representatives of reserved tribal seats, and only two of ex-untouchable, showed up among my link members; due proportion would have been 3 and 7, respectively. Moreover, the reserved seat vote is overwhelmingly Congress. The leader in Parliament of the ex-untouchable party succeeded himself in winning a general seat. "I get more done for my people than all of the sheep the Congress brings in through reserved seats," he told me. It sounds like what the first Scots labor representative might have said about Dundas, the shepherd of the 45 Scottish votes in the eighteenth-century British Parliament. Yet probably to keep these votes docile, Congress or any government will have to maintain, even accelerate, the employment of these subject people in government. It is a majestic achievement of the movement of Gandhi and Nehru that they found constitutional forms, justifiable by universal norms, for a system of *cooptative* representation like that which merged the Scottish into the British elite.

But India has to integrate all its many peoples with the nation-building leadership. The job seems to me much too big to be accomplished by coopting the bottom and the periphery of society and leaving the peasant middle to virtual representation, while influential representation is developed by opposition parties in the constituencies of greatest conflict and dissent.

Building and Shedding Government Responsibilities

Having consolidated itself, a national leadership undertakes increasing responsibilities. This gives occasion for opposition parties, originating from policy cleavage in parliament, to mobilize social cleavages of nationwide extent.

The load of the British government dropped during the first half of the eighteenth century (with Walpole it was conscious policy, both domestic and foreign) but was resumed and dramatically enlarged first on the colonial scene and then domestically, after the national ruling elite was consolidated. The party split (the lasting one which connected constituencies to alternative sets of leaders) came upon dissatisfaction with the conduct of those larger responsibilities.

India appears to be going through the same enlargement of the agenda of government. The national budget expands in relation to the national income, industries are nationalized, the model is the "welfare state" and a "socialist pattern of society." That is the appearance. To Gunnar Myrdal, whose reference is to a Northern European tradition of governmental responsibility for social welfare, India is a "soft state."[40] It lacks the very ability which Britain developed early in its national existence to decide and carry through measures which allocate benefits and burdens. There is much evidence to support Myrdal's diagnosis, indeed, to sharpen it. Basic reforms have been decided as national policy (e.g., land reform or cooperative farming) outside Parliament's legislative procedure. These reforms have then been evaded or neglected. The Planning Commission under Nehru might be seen as a way of relieving politicians of, and embarrassing economists with, allocations of the major public investments.

In any event, I have some evidence for the present weight of national government activities in the national representative process. I asked the MPs what types of demands were put to them by constituents. Of 184 who responded, 105 listed one or more subjects within national responsibility, 78 listed only matters dealt with by state or local governments, one listed only grievances of his "community" (that is his tribe, religious group, caste, or linguistic minority) without reference to any governmental action. I asked for the list in order of frequency, and here the results are surprising. Eleven Members got "communal" demands most frequently; 149 got subjects of state or local governmental concern; only 24 got national demands.

The national government has not, then, been doing enough to evoke a widespread reaction among constituents. The divisions and decisions in the Indian Parliament have, instead, been of three main kinds. There have been controversies over the ideology or the shares of power among the Westernized intelligentsia (e.g., nonalignment in foreign affairs, nationalization of large-scale banking). There have been paper policies of modest or radical social redistribution (Compulsory Deposits, ceilings on farm size and redistribution of the surplus among tenants, cooperative farming) which were not effected precisely because they threatened to change the daily lives of a large proportion of Indian families. There were sectional claims of culturally defined states (linguistic boundaries for states, Kashmir, the Tamil language). In this third type of decision, resistance came from political movements already entrenched regionally. If the Indian leadership had been insensitive (which it was not) as well as indecisive (which it was) we could find the British analogue in Ireland, not Scotland.

There are exceptions. Industrial relations policy is one, but in an agrarian nation it affects only about 10 percent of the population. Food supply and food prices have created what were potentially the most penetrating national issues. In the years of scarcity, however, the government of India let each state become a separate food market. The load was shed.

CONCLUSIONS

Comparison in the time dimension has revealed something, even for societies so disparate as Britain and India. The eighteenth-century British Parliament and the contemporary Indian are both policy arenas normally insulated from what Plumb called "an amorphous mass of political sentiment" outside, which finds expression in "occasional hysteria and impotent polemic." But in both, Parliament shows power to warn of impending limits to the people's toleration and to reinforce that warning with election losses or losses of Government majorities. Adult suffrage makes much less difference in either respect than we would have supposed. Suffrage does probably accelerate the political education of the more fragmented and parochial Indian village population. It puts down more ladders for ambitious men of however diverse origin to climb toward a national elite. But it has shown no power to generate an elite where history provided no "sense of common identity in those who wielded economic, social, and political power."

So much for the static perspective. The second and more penetrating insight we derived from our comparison through time was of a developmental sequence. After a century of civil war and contested legitimacy, English power to govern was fused in the hands of a unified but moderate elite. It used power to push both economic and colonial expansion. At last, through a colonial war burdening most families, a split came. That was between fifty and seventy-five years after the elite had consolidated its rule. The split deepened to a permanent party competition, broadening its base as it fed upon lasting differences of constituency interests. The Indian sequence, so far, is otherwise. Divisions thrust down to the villages by electoral competition weakened the base of leadership. We can speculate, to be sure, that in twenty years of power the Congress Party might have built a party machine to fill by organization and cooptation the weakness of the national elite. Nehru, however, was preoccupied with policy, not power. His models were twentieth century, not eighteenth. And while he could be replaced as prime minister, as arbiter of splits among the ruling elements he left neither an individual nor institutional successor.

Time comparison has shown us its limits, too. Federalism, India's main device for governing a multicultural nation, was unknown to Walpole's generation, unknown, indeed, until the American experiment half a century later. Again, we can speculate that a British federal solution might have made Catholic Ireland safe for the United Kingdom. But by that time history had almost preempted the option: "Home Rule means Rome Rule." To be sure, federalism in its political (as against its constitutional) meaning, is almost as difficult for the heirs of empire and of the Indian national liberation movement. It is the failure of Congress governments in the states to deliver on social reforms to which the Congress government in Delhi committed them which has given opposition parties in India their most obvious openings. Yet federalism remains a last resort to the dividing leadership; it is one that might lighten their load to match their declining powers of decision.

There is one respect, finally, in which no nation has available to it the precise developmental sequence of its predecessors. Thoroughly overlaying her eighteenth-century heritage, India inevitably received the hard-earned lessons and the institutional innovations of nineteenth- and twentieth-century Europe. Personal rule was parceled out to plural institutions, civil service replaced patronage, public was sorted from private power, self-government came finally to be defined as the competition of parties for the votes of all. While the personnel and institutions of rule were thus being conscientiously divided, some higher authority was keeping order: the external power of an integrated and industrialized Britain up to 1947, the internal power of the Gandhian moral crusade for twenty years more.

Whether India can learn that self-government means accepting some common authority without passing through some counterpart of the British sixteenth century our scheme of comparison cannot tell us. To this degree, building a nation and a government legitimate for it remains a lonely adventure.

N O T E S

1. Lok Sabha Debates, 3d Series, Vol. 1, Col. 25 (April 17, 1962).
2. *Ibid.,* Col. 51.
3. *Nationalism and Social Communication* (Cambridge, Mass.: Massachusetts Institute of Technology Press, 1963).
4. Population estimates for years between 1750 and 1755 are given in Brian R. Mitchell and Phyllis Deane, *Abstract of British Historical Statistics* (Cambridge: The University Press, 1962), p. 5: England and Wales 6.2 million, Scotland 1.2 million, Ireland 3.0 million. Wales had perhaps 0.5 million.
5. Gwynfor Evans and Ioan Rhys, "Wales," in Owen Dudley Edwards, et al., *Celtic Nationalism* (London: Routledge and Kegan Paul, 1968), pp. 232–233.
6. *Ibid.,* pp. 234–235.
7. Lewis Namier and John Brooke, *The History of Parliament: The House of Commons 1754–1790,* vol. 1 (London: Her Majesty's Stationery Office, 1964), pp. 175–176.
8. Marjory A. Bald, "Anglicization of Scottish Printing," *Scottish Historical Review,* 23 (1925–26), 107–115, and "Pioneers of Anglicized Speech in Scotland," *Ibid.,* 24 (1926–27), 179–193.
9. See Andrew Browning, ed., *English Historical Documents 1660– 1714* (New York: Oxford University Press, 1953), vol. 8, pp. 680–695.
10. *The Origins of Political Stability in England, 1675–1725* (Boston: Houghton Mifflin, 1967), p. xviii.
11. *Ibid.,* p. 69.
12. For this aspect of Parliament's work, see Samuel H. Beer, *British Politics in the Collectivist Age* (New York: Knopf, 1965), pp. 25 ff.
13. *The Origins of Political Stability in England,* chap. 4.
14. *Ibid.,* p. 134.
15. *Ibid.,* p. 19.
16. J. H. Plumb, et al., *Man versus Society in Eighteenth-Century Britain* (Cambridge: The University Press, 1968), p. 2.

17. Plumb, *Political Stability,* p. 29.
18. Edward Porritt, *The Unreformed House of Commons* (Cambridge: The University Press, 1903), p. 13.
19. Plumb, *Political Stability,* p. 95.
20. Keith Grahame Feiling, *The Second Tory Party, 1714–1832* (London: Macmillan, 1938), p. 24.
21. Ivor Jennings, *Party Politics,* vol. II, *The Growth of Parties* (Cambridge: The University Press, 1961), pp. 27–28.
22. Plumb, *Political Stability,* p. 135.
23. Aristide R. Zolberg, *Creating Political Order* (Chicago: Rand McNally, 1966), chap. V, p. 160.
24. "Political Man," in his *Man versus Society in Eighteenth-Century Britain,* p. 12.
25. *Ibid.,* p. 10.
26. Plumb, *Political Stability,* p. 185.
27. Namier and Brooke, *The History of Parliament,* p. 71.
28. *Man versus Society,* p. 13.
29. Feiling, *The Second Tory Party* p. 56.
30. *Political Parties and Political Development* (Princeton, N.J.: Princeton University Press, 1966), p. 27.
31. *Party Systems and Voter Alignments* (New York: The Free Press, 1967), p. 36.
32. Peter D. G. Thomas, "The Beginnings of Parliamentary Reporting in Newspapers, 1768–1774," *English Historical Review,* 74 (1959), 623–636.
33. Namier and Brooke, *The History of Parliament,* pp. 68, 74, 184, 190, 196, 199.
34. See, e.g., Commonwealth Parliamentary Association, *Report of Proceedings, Twelfth Commonwealth Parliamentary Conference* (London: The Association, 1966), p. 98.
35. Michael Brecher, *Succession in India, a Study in Decision-Making* (London: Oxford University Press, 1966).
36. *India, the Most Dangerous Decades* (Princeton, N.J.: Princeton University Press, 1960).
37. Choice of the nominees for President has not been so regularized, though it, too, has nation-building significance.
38. J. H. Broomfield, "The Regional Elites: A Theory of Modern Indian History," *Indian Economic and Social History Review,* 3 (1966), 279–291, and subsequent books by Broomfield and Irschick.
39. My sampling bias, overweighting oppositionists busy in the Parliament itself, probably weakened a still stronger contrast in this respect.
40. *Asian Drama, an Inquiry into the Poverty of Nations* (New York: Pantheon, 1968), vol 2, pp. 895 ff.

7

Policy Demands and System Support: The Role of the Represented

J O H N C . W A H L K E

*Conflicting expectations of parliament, born of contrasting ex-
periences across nations and over time, have caused controversies
not only among interested observers but also among relatively
dispassionate scholars. Political scientists disagree not so much
about what parliament should do, but what in fact it does. In
the selection below, John C. Wahlke, one of the leading students
of legislative behavior, says that political scientists have spent
too much time studying the policy-making function of legislatures to the exclusion of their "supportive" functions. He considers this the result of an outworn conception of representation
which regards representatives as merely the policy-making agents
of their constituents and fails to consider the possible influence
of the representatives on those whom they represent. Wahlke
therefore proposes a reconceptualization of representation which
would lead legislative research to take account of the role of
legislatures in building consent and sustaining political order.
Such an approach promises a substantial reassessment of the
function of representative assemblies in the political system.*

Discontent with the functioning of representative
bodies is hardly new. Most were born and developed in the face

This chapter is a revision of a paper originally presented to the Seventh World
Congress of the International Political Science Association, September 1967,
and published in *The British Journal of Political Science,* 1 (1971). It is reprinted by permission of the author and the publisher.

of opposition denying their legitimacy and their feasibility.[1] Most have lived amid persistent unfriendly attitudes, ranging from the total hostility of antidemocrats to the pessimistic assessments of such diverse commentators as Lord Bryce, Walter Lippmann, and Charles de Gaulle.[2] Of particular interest today is the discontent with representative bodies expressed by the friends of democracy, the supporters of representative government, many of whom see in recent history a secular "decline of parliament" and in prospect the imminent demise of representative bodies.[3]

Much of the pessimism among the friends of representative government appears, however, to be very poorly grounded. The notion that we are witnessing the "decline of parliament," it has been observed, "has never been based on careful inquiry into the function of parliaments in their presumed golden age, nor into their subsequent performance."[4] Neither has it rested on careful inquiry into the functions and roles of citizens, individually and collectively, in a representative democracy. Indeed, it is both possible and likely that, "If there is a crisis . . . it is a crisis in the theory of representation and not in the institution of representation."[5] This paper suggests how (and why) we might begin to reformulate representation theory and to identify the critical questions which research must answer.

DEMAND-INPUT CONCEPTS OF REPRESENTATION

Much of the disillusionment and dissatisfaction with modern representative government grows out of a fascination with the policy decisions of representative bodies which, in turn, reflects what may be called a "policy-demand-input" conception of government in general and the representative processes in particular. Theorists and researchers alike have long taken it for granted that the problem of representative government centers on the linkage between citizens' policy preferences and the public-policy decisions of representative bodies. Almost without exception they have conceived of the public side of this relationship in terms of "demands" and the assembly side in terms of "responses." Julius Turner, for instance, has said that "the representative process in twentieth-century America involves . . . the attempt of the representative to mirror the political *desires* of those groups which can bring about his election or defeat."[6] Almond and Verba, in the course of explicating new dimensions of civic behavior (to which we shall return) take the making of demands to be the characteristic act of citizens in democratic systems: "The competent citizen has a role in the formation of general policy. Furthermore, he plays an *influential* role in this decision-making process: he participates through the use of explicit or implicit threats of some form of deprivation if the official does not comply with his demands."[7]

The Simple Demand-Input Model

The basic elements in the general policy-demand-input conception can be described, in necessarily oversimplified form, as follows. The principal force in a representative system is (as it ought to be) the conscious desires and wishes of citizens, frequently examined in modern research on representation under the heading of "interests." Interests are thought of as constituting "policy demands" or "policy expectations," and the governmental process seems to "begin" with citizens exerting them on government. Government, in this view, is essentially a process for discovering policies which will maximally meet the policy expectations of citizens. There are several points at which emphases or interpretations may vary in important respects, but the critical assumptions of this view and the points at which such variations may occur can readily be outlined.

In the first place, the interests which constitute the fundamental stuff of democratic, representative politics are most often thought of in terms of specific policy opinions or attitudes, i.e., preference or dislike for particular courses of government action. But it is also common to envision citizens holding less specific policy preferences in the form of ideological orientations or belief systems.

Although "interests" are taken to be rooted in individual desires, they may be expressed in the form of either individual policy opinions (often aggregated by opinion analysts as "public opinion" or the opinion of some segment of the public) or organized group (associational) opinion, usually thought to be expressed on behalf of the individuals by group agents or spokesmen, or, of course, in both forms simultaneously.

Analytically, the core of the representative process is the communication of these various forms of interest to governmental actors, which is thought to occur in either or both of two principal ways. It may take place through constituency influence, i.e., the communication of aggregated individual views by constituents to their "representatives." (The latter term theoretically includes administrative agency personnel, police officials, judges, and countless other governmental actors, but we shall deal here only with members of representative bodies.) Communication may also occur through group pressure or lobbying activities, conceived of as communication by group agents who are intermediaries between representatives and the aggregates of citizens for whom they (the group agents) speak.

The critical process for making representative government democratically responsible is, of course, election of the representatives. Elections are the indispensable mechanism for ensuring a continuing linkage between citizens' public-policy views (interests) and the public policy formulated by representatives (in cooperation, needless to say, with executives and administrators). The mechanism works in one or both of two ways. It may provide representatives with a mandate to enact into public policy at an early date the policy views expressed in the elections. It may also serve to legitimize, by stamping the *imprimatur* of citizen acceptance on, the policies most recently enacted by the representatives.

However logical and obvious such a conception of democratic representative governmental processes may seem, the observed behavior of citizens is in almost all critical respects inconsistent with it. Some of the more important established propositions about observed behavior which conflict with assumptions about the role of policy-demand inputs in politics may be listed here, even though there is no room to list in detail the evidence supporting them. They are, in most instances, propositions which are well known, although not normally brought to bear in discussions of representation:[8]

(1) Few citizens entertain interests that clearly represent "policy demands" or "policy expectations" or wishes and desires that are readily convertible into them.

(2) Few people even have thought-out, consistent, and firmly held positions on most matters of public policy.

(3) It is highly doubtful that policy demands are entertained even in the form of broad orientations, outlooks, or belief systems.

(4) Large proportions of citizens lack the instrumental knowledge about political structures, processes, and actors that they would need to communicate policy demands or expectations if they had any.

(5) Relatively few citizens communicate with their representatives.

(6) Citizens are not especially interested or informed about the policy-making activities of their representatives as such.

(7) Nor are citizens much interested in other day-to-day aspects of parliamentary functioning.

(8) Relatively few citizens have any clear notion that they are making policy demands or policy choices when they vote.

None of this, of course, is new or surprising information. But it is sometimes forgotten when working from slightly less naïve models of the representational system than the one sketched out above. Each of the alternative models familiar to students of representative bodies, however, must sooner or later reckon with these facts.

A Responsible-Party Model

Whatever else they are doing in the electoral process, voters in most political systems are certainly choosing between candidates advanced by political parties. It is therefore easy to assume that electoral choice between party candidates is the vehicle for making policy choices and to derive logically plausible mechanisms by which that choice might be made. For such mechanisms of demand-input to operate, several requirements would have to be met. In the first place, there must be a formulated party program and it must be known to the voters. Second, representatives' policy-making behavior must reflect that program. Third, voters must identify candidates with programs and legislative records, and base their choices on reaction to them.[9] The arguments against the American party system and in favor of the British on grounds of systemic capacity for meeting these requirements are well known.[10]

In most American contexts, the failure of party and legislative personnel to provide appropriate policy cues makes the applicability of the responsible-party model dubious to begin with, no matter what voters might be doing. But there are also signs of voter failure to respond appropriately to whatever such cues might be available. In one American state (Washington), for example, far less than half the public knew which party controlled either house of the state legislature at its most recent session (41 percent in the case of the lower, 27 percent for the upper house).[11] Shortly after the 1966 election in the United States, 31 percent of the electorate did not know (or was wrong about) which party had a majority in Congress just before the election; more striking still, 34 percent did not know which party had won most seats in that election and another 45 percent misinterpreted Republican gains to believe the Republican Party had won a majority![12] With respect to public reaction to party at the national level, Miller and Stokes have demonstrated that party symbols are almost devoid of policy content, which is not surprising in view of what they call the legislative party "cacophony."[13] And Converse, in one of the few relevant studies using panel data, found that party identification was far more stable among American voters sampled in 1958 and 1960 than their opinions on any "issues."[14] We can only conclude, at least for the American case, that, with or without policy content, party symbols do not serve the American voter as the responsible-party model would wish.

Of somewhat greater interest, however, is the situation in those countries where it seems more likely that party and legislative leaders provide voters the conditions under which they could, if they chose, behave as the responsible-party model would have them. The British political system is usually cited as the classic example. What, then, are the facts about the connection between voting and policy preferences of British voters? Perhaps because it has been so commonly taken for granted that every general election in Britain constitutes an electoral mandate or at least an unfavorable judgment on past policy performance, surprisingly little evidence is available. The most direct testimony, from a nationwide survey of 1960, is that, given a question asking them to differentiate between the two major parties with respect to sixteen political ends or party traits, on only four of the statements did as many as two-thirds of the sample attribute a clear-cut goal to either party, and these were not stated in policy but in group (e.g., "middle class") or personal terms; on four, some one-half or more were unaware of any difference between the parties, and on the remaining eight, between 33 percent and 45 percent detected no differences.[15] There is strong reason, then, to doubt the applicability of the responsible-party model even in Great Britain.

But the most persuasive reason for questioning that model is what we know about the phenomenon of party identification itself. For the mere fact that one political party (or coalition) is replaced in government by another as a result of changing electoral fortunes, together with the fact that voters are making electoral choices between parties, does not in itself demonstrate anything at all about the relationship between election results and the public's views about party programs or policy stands. There is abundant evidence, on the contrary, that in many political systems voters identify with a political party much as they identify with a baseball or soccer team. Many voters in many lands are better described as "rooters," team supporters, than as policy advocates or program evaluators. The authors of *The American Voter* have acquainted us with the importance of that phenomenon in the United States.[16] Of special interest here is their finding that, far from serving as a vehicle for the voter to express prior formed policy views, it is more likely that "party loyalty plays no small role in the formation of attitudes on specific policy matters."[17] More recent studies seem to show that party identification of German voters is in some respects similar.[18] The very great stability of party loyalties in Great Britain suggests strongly the operation of similar mechanisms there: "Not many people switch their votes in the course of their whole lives; therefore, the number changing in the short period between any two successive elections is necessarily small. On this definition, only 4 percent of the electors in the Bristol sample [Bristol Northeast, 1951] were floaters. . . ."[19]

It can hardly be said, then, that the responsible-party model solves any of the theoretical problems encountered in the elementary atomistic model of representative democracy. If anything, it raises further and more serious ones.

Polyarchal and Elitist Models

Historically, the awareness that few humans are politically involved or active was at the core of many antidemocratic theories. More recently it has been the starting assumption for various elitist conceptions of power structure, particularly at the level of local communities.[20] Still more recently the empirical accuracy of the assumption as well as the justifiability of "elitist" conclusions drawn from it have been questioned and subjected to empirical research.[21]

Our concern here is not with the general theoretical problems raised by such approaches, however.[22] It is rather with their implications for the demand-input conception of representative processes. The chief implication, of course, is that policy demands and policy expectations are manifested by a relative few and not by citizens in general. This implication is hardly to be questioned. Summarizing relevant knowledge on the point, one recent article notes that "Most recent academic studies of public attitudes . . . indicate differences between the political attitudes of elite groups and attitudes reflected in mass samples."[23] And Converse and Dupeux have said that "It appears likely that the more notable [Franco-American] differences stem from the actions of elites and require study and explanation primarily at this level, rather than at the level of the mass electorate."[24]

The crucial question, then, concerns the extent to which and the mechanisms by which elites' policy-demanding activities are connected to the representational activities of the mass public. One possibility is that there is competition for different policy satisfactions among different elites, that this competition is settled initially in the governmental process, much as Latham has described the group process:

> The principal function of official groups is to provide various levels of compromise in the writing of the rules, within the body of agreed principles that forms the consensus upon which the political community rests. In so performing this function, each of the three principal branches of government has a special role.
>
> The legislature referees the group struggle, ratifies the victories of the successful coalitions, and records the terms of the surrenders, compromises, and conquests in the form of statutes.[25]

What Latham leaves unsaid is how members of the voting public enter into this process "within the body of agreed principles that forms the consensus upon which the political community rests." Does it, by electoral decision, provide the ultimate ratification of policies formulated in the process of compromise among elites (groups)? At the very most, one might look for some "potential" power in the hands of the general public which it could use, if it wished, to ratify or reject policies and programs thus put before it. But all the considerations which made the simple atomistic and responsible-party conceptions implausible apply with equal force and in identical fashion against such an interpretation. Thus, when we look for public participation through electoral choice among competing elites, we encounter the same difficulties we have encountered before. So-called polyarchal or elite-democracy models are no more helpful in connecting policy-making to policy demands from the public than were the atomistic and party models.

THE CONCEPT OF THE RESPONSIBLE REPRESENTATIVE

Demand-input emphases have tended also to color our views of what constitutes responsible behavior by elected representatives. Since the kind of findings just surveyed are well known, few modern studies consider Edmund Burke's "instructed delegate model" appropriate for modern legislators.[26] Most report without surprise the lack of connection between any sort of policy-demand input from the citizenry and the policy-making behavior of representatives.

Nevertheless, most studies of representative behavior accept the premise that conformity between legislators' actions and the public's policy views is the central problem of representative government, usually envisioning some kind of role conception or normative mechanism through which the agreement comes about. Thus Jewell and Patterson argue that high concern of representatives for their constituency is plausible in spite of the fact that legislators have low saliency in constituents' eyes.[27] And Miller and Stokes suggest still more specifically that, in spite of these facts, "the idea of reward or punishment at the polls for legislative stands is familiar to members of Congress, who feel that they and their records are quite visible to their constituents."[28] A recent study by John Kingdon suggests one interesting mechanism through which the moral obligation to represent constituency views might work: what he terms the "congratulation-rationalization effect" leads winners of Congressional elections to have higher estimates of voters' interest and information than do losers and to attribute less importance to party label and more importance to policy issues in voters' actions at their election than do losers. Therefore:

> The incumbent is more likely than if he lost to believe that voters are watching him, that they are better informed, and that they make their own choices according to his own characteristics and even according to the issues of the election. Because of the congratulation-rationalization effect . . . [he] may pay greater attention to the constituency than otherwise, because he believes that his constituents are paying greater attention to him than he might think if he had lost.[29]

Perhaps the most persuasive explanation of the mechanism linking public views to legislative policy is that offered by Miller and Stokes. They compared representatives' votes in several policy domains to constituency opinion, representatives' personal opinion, and representatives' perceptions of their constituency's opinion in order to determine the proportionate contribution of each to his voting. In brief, they found that constituency policy views play a large role for Congressmen in civil rights issues but a negligible role in domestic welfare issues. Cnudde and McCrone, extending this line of research, demonstrated the primary importance of the Congressman's perceptions of his constituents' opinions in establishing whatever link there is from constituency through to legislative voting. That is, in civil rights issues, Congressmen appear to shape their attitudes to fit the opinions they think their constituency holds.[30]

These findings, while in some respects striking, are nonetheless ambiguous. From the standpoint of our understanding of representative government, the results of studies of the behavior of representatives are as unsatisfactory as the studies of citizen behavior seem disquieting. Many questions are left unanswered, theoretically or empirically. Often the differences on which theoretically important distinctions are based are found to be small. Above all, in spite of the fact that legislative policy decisions are universally taken to be the most important type of legislative output, we know almost nothing about the character, let alone the conditions and causes, of how they vary in content. We now turn briefly to this problem.

Socioeconomic Determinants of Policy

"Policies" have been described as the most important variety of political output, and legislative policy decisions are commonly understood to be the most important type of legislative output.[31] It has been argued, therefore, that a major problem for legislative research is "to achieve adequate conceptualization of legislative output, i.e., to specify the dimensions or variables of legislative output which are related to different consequences of that output."[32] So it is rather startling to discover that the term "policy" remains almost totally unconceptualized, i.e., that the literature provides "no theoretically meaningful categories which distinguish between types of policies."[33]

There is, however, a recent series of methodologically sophisticated but theoretically unstructured inquiries into possible variations in public policy which tends still further to challenge the relevance of demand-input conceptions to understanding the representative process. Most of these studies utilize the readily available masses of quantitative data about American states to analyze relationships among policy outputs and many possible correlates. Variations in policy output have usually been measured by the amount of money spent by a system on different categories of substantive policy or program, such as public highways, health programs, welfare, etc. Political variables investigated have usually been "structural" in nature—for example, degree of two-party competition, degree of voter participation, extent of legislative malapportionment, and so on. Socioeconomic environmental (or "background") variables have included such things as degree of urbanization and industrialization and level of education.

It is the general import of these studies that, with only rare and minor exceptions, variations in public policy are *not* related to variations in political-structure variables, except insofar as socioeconomic or environmental variables affect them and public policy variations together. Variations in policy output can be almost entirely "explained" (in the statistical sense) by environmental variables, without reference to the variables supposedly reflecting different systems and practices of representation. Most far-reaching of such studies is Dye's examination of the effects of economic development (industrialization, urbanization, income, education) and political system (party division, party competition, political participation, and malapportionment) on ninety policy variables in four different policy fields. He concludes that "system characteristics have relatively little *independent* effect on policy outcomes in the states. Economic development shapes both political systems and policy outcomes, and most of the association that occurs between system characteristics and policy outcomes can be attributed to the influence of economic development."[34]

It is possible, of course, that these remarkable findings are unique to the American political system. That such is not the case, however, is strongly suggested by Cutright's discovery that variations in the national security programs of seventy-six nations appear to be directly explainable in terms of economic-development level and to be unrelated to differences in ideology or type of political system (including differences between communist and capitalist systems).[35] There is a curious hint of similar findings in a study suggesting that changes in foreign policy do not seem to be associated with instances of "leadership succession" so far as voting in the UN General Assembly is concerned; that is, there is apparently substantial continuity of foreign policy in any given system despite changes in political regime.[36]

In sum, then, the policy-environment correlation studies imply that stimuli which have been thought to be policy demands are really just automatically determined links in a chain of reactions from environment to policy output, a chain in which neither policy demands, policy expectations, nor any other kind of policy orientation plays any significant role. There is no room, in other words, for any of the policy-related behaviors and attitudes of citizens which we examined in the preceding section of this paper to enter into the policy process.

THE INFLUENCE OF REPRESENTATION ON THE REPRESENTED

The foregoing arguments are not especially "antidemocratic" or "antirepresentative." They are just as damaging to much antidemocratic theory and to elitist criticisms of representative democracy. It is not only policy opinions of citizens in the mass public which are demoted in the rank order of policy determinants but policy opinions of elites and group leaderships as well. The principal implication is that "policy-process" studies whose aim is primarily to discover the political bases of policy decisions conceived of as choices between policy alternatives contended for by divergent political forces, or to explain why a particular decision went one way instead of another, comprehend too little of the political life of man and that the part they do comprehend is probably not its most vital. The appropriate conclusion is not the grandiose notion that representative democracy is chimerical but the limited recognition that our conceptions of government, politics, and representation are somehow deficient, that "policy-making" plays a different and evidently smaller role in the governance of society than we thought.

Precisely what role we cannot yet say, for neglecting to study the political consequences of policy-making is "a practice very much in line with the tradition of political science."[37] Research on representation has tended toward preoccupation with the results of legislative roll calls and other decisions or the results of elections and series of elections. It has concentrated on the antecedents of legislative "output" and left unexamined the political "outcomes" which above all make output an appropriate object of political study.[38] It has explored the possible sources of variations as small as a few percentage points in the influence of "factors" influencing legislative and electoral decision but ignored the relationship, if any, between legislative output and the incidence of discontent, riots, wars, civil wars, coups d'etat, revolutions, and decay or integration of human groups. Its focus has been determined by "political theories of allocation," in almost total disregard of the perspectives opened up by "theories of systems persistence."[39] This is an essential part of de Jouvenel's charge that political science has not so far had the "dangerous" impact it might because it has so far been content to investigate only "weak political behavior."[40]

A plausible working hypothesis which directs the study of representation toward "strong political behavior" is provided by Easton's discussion of "support." Viewed from this perspective, previous studies are seen to presume that political systems stand, fall, or change according to the "specific support" accorded them, the "consent" granted "as a consequence from some specific satisfaction obtained from the system with respect to a demand that the members make."[41] But the arguments above show that specific support, the support attaching directly to citizens' reactions to policy decisions, does not adequately describe the relationship between citizen and government. We must also recognize and take into account what Easton calls "diffuse support," the support constituted by "generalized attachment to political objects . . . not conditioned upon specific returns at any moment."[42]

There is good warrant for the working hypothesis that:

Except in the long run, diffuse support is independent of the effects of daily outputs. It consists of a reserve of support that enables a system to weather the many storms when outputs cannot be balanced off against inputs of demands. It is a kind of support that a system does not have to buy with more or less direct benefits for the obligations and responsibilities the member incurs. If we wish, the outputs here may be considered psychic or symbolic, and in this sense, they may offer the individual immediate benefits strong enough to stimulate a supportive response.[43]

The plausibility of such a starting point has been intimated by other observers. Edelman's instructive discussion of the importance of "symbolic" as compared with "instrumental" satisfactions deriving from the administration of public policies clearly argues for it.[44] More directly concerning representative functions, Thomas Anton has shown, with respect to the roles of agency spokesmen, budget officers, legislators, and citizens in the budgetary process of American states, that "what is at stake . . . is not so much the distribution of resources, about which state actors have little to say, but the distribution of symbolic satisfaction among the involved actors and the audiences which observe their stylized behavior."[45] And Alfred de Grazia has discussed the ways in which "the election process is symbolic and psychological in meaning, rather than a device for the purpose of instructing delegates."[46]

That the problem of support is a proper springboard for representation research is suggested also by some commentators on the functions of representative bodies. Almost thirty years ago, T. V. Smith spoke of the "cathartic function" of legislatures, which by themselves appearing as scapegoats, harmlessly conduct away disaffections that otherwise "might well totalize into attacks upon public order."[47] More recently, Eulau and Hinckley have pointed out that representative bodies perform "such latent functions . . . as consensus-building, interest aggregation, catharsis for anxieties and resentment, the crystallization and resolution of conflicts, and the legitimization of decisions made elesewhere in the political system."[48] With respect to Great Britain, Beer has described the main parliamentary task as that of "mobilizing consent . . . certainly not the representative function by which in greater or lesser degree the legislature brings the grievances and wishes of the people to bear upon policy-making."[49] And Patterson has asserted that "A legislature is much more than a law-making factory. It is a symbol of representative, democratic government. Its symbolic 'output' may be related to the kinds of policies it makes, but it is related also to the representative adequacy of the legislature, to the respect citizens can have for individual legislators, and to the pride citizens can take in their legislatures."[50] David Truman has drawn important implications from such a view for the behavior of representatives, arguing that the primary skill lying at the heart of representative government is not substantive, technical skill, but in combination with that, "a special skill. This is skill in assaying what is asked or done in the name of substantive expertise and in reconciling or combining such claims or acts with the feasibilities that exist or can be created in the electorate, in the extragovernmental world in all its configurations."[51]

The shift of attention from "demands" to "support" which all these insights suggest calls for a corresponding shift of research emphasis from the behavior of representatives, which has hitherto preoccupied most of us, to the perceptions, attitudes, and behaviors of the people whom representatives collectively represent, about which as yet we really know very little. The most immediate task is a primarily conceptual one—to identify the dimensions of support behavior, to map the incidence and variations of support in specific systems, and, through comparative analysis of support mechanisms in different systems, to formulate hypotheses about its conditions and correlates.

THE SUPPORTIVE FUNCTIONS OF REPRESENTATION

David Easton's definition of support as affective orientation toward political objects and his analytical distinction of political community, political regime, and political authorities as the three principal categories of such political objects is a useful starting point.[52] We can probably assume, to begin with, that support

for the political community is the most pervasive, general (diffuse), and stable element in the overall support mechanism of
any political system. Basic group identification, the sort of "pre-
political" sentiment giving all segments of the community a
"we-feeling . . . not that they are just a group but that they are
a political entity that works together and will likely share a common political fate and destiny,"[53] is surely a major dimension of
this level of support. Everything we know about the historical
evolution of nation-states, tribal societies, and all other political
forms, as well as everything modern research tells us about the
processes of political socialization, indicates that the loyalties,
identifications, and cognitive-affective structures which make up
this communal-loyalty dimension are acquired and shaped in
early childhood and are affected little, if at all, by any political
events, let alone such little salient events as the functioning of
representative bodies. The indispensability of this kind of support for any political system was noted by V. O. Key: "A basic
prerequisite is that the population be pervaded by a national loyalty. Or perhaps, more accurately, that the population not consist
of segments each with its own sense of separateness."[54] Almond
and Verba, whose concept of "systems affect" approximates the
concept of support for political community, likewise appear to
take for granted (at least in the five countries they studied) the
existence of a nationality sentiment or similar community sense
defining a political community toward which members respond
with varying effect.[55]

But what if no sentiment of political community binds together a group of people who are, in fact, being governed (as is
the case in many new African nations, to give an obvious example)? Or if segments seem increasingly to develop "each with its
own sense of separateness" (as may well be the case in Canada
or Belgium)? Can we be sure that the "sense of community must
also be in part a product of public policy?"[56] If not "policy,"
what aspect then of governmental activity, and especially of representative bodies' activity, affects it? At this stage we can only
wonder—and begin to design research to find out.

A second major dimension of political community support is suggested by Almond and Verba's typology of political cultures, comprising what we may interpret as the political roles of "parochial," "subject," and "participant." The authors' original formulation differentiates these three types primarily in terms of their relative participation in demand-input activities.[57] There is justification even in the original formulation, however, for viewing these roles as differentiated also by the extent of conscious support for the political community, or the "gradation from 'public' to 'private' ": "The overwhelming majority of the members of all political systems live out their lives, discover, develop, and express their feelings and aspirations in the intimate groups of the community. It is the rare individual who is fully recruited into the political system and becomes a political man."[58] Viewed this way, the second component of community support, which might be labeled "political commitment," appears as an autonomously defined political variable, a kind of participation through sensitivity and alertness to political events and objects as well as participation in civic and political roles—participation in politics per se, not necessarily in the sense of power seeking, however, and not participation in primarily instrumental activities. It is a kind of "political interest," but "it is interest not in the form of gains in material well-being, power, or status, but it is rather in personal satisfaction and growth attained from active engagement in the political process."[59]

A number of familiar concepts bear on this second dimension of political-community support. Most of the phenomena usually treated under the heading of "political alienation," for example, represent an extreme negative value, ranking above only such antisupportive positions as rebellion itself. "Political apathy," in a sense related to Almond and Verba's "parochialism," is more supportive than alienation but less so than "compliance." More supportive still is active "interest and involvement," although one must be careful to remember that support for the political community here is perfectly compatible (perhaps often associated?) with failure of support for regime or authorities. Beyond active spectator interest there is participation of varying degrees—ranging from nothing more than sporadic voting to regular and intensive political communication, to participation in authority or other "trans-civic" roles.

Such a conception of supportive political commitment seems perfectly consistent with what we do know about the relevant behavior of citizens. For example, once-depressing statistics about "low levels" of citizen interest take on quite different meaning in this light. The finding that "only" 27 percent of the American public could be considered politically active,[60] that during 1945 and 1946 sometimes "as few as" 19 percent and "never more than" 36 percent of the American Zone population in West Germany claimed to be personally interested in politics,[61] that in 1958 35 percent of the West Germans had no interest at all in attending Bundestag sessions even if it cost them nothing,[62] or the countless similar readings of political interest and involvement in other political systems, must now, if there is no other different evidence on the point, be read not as sure signs of "apathy" or "negativism" but as probable indications of moderate support for the political community.

Still, on balance, we know much less than we should about the dynamics of support for the political community. Though we can recognize that communal loyalty and political commitment constitute important dimensions of it, we do not know how one dimension relates to the other, or how the day-to-day functioning of government, including the input-output functioning of representative institutions, relates to either.

The situation is not much different when we consider the problem of support for the "political regime." One major dimension here appears to be the level of conscious support for broad norms and values which apply to the political world generally, i.e., to "rules of the game," or standards by which regimes are judged. But the meaning of what information we have here is ambiguous. How much consensus, in the sense of "agreement on fundamentals," may vary, and what is the effect of such variation, are questions which do not yet have clear answers.[63]

The level of support for the institutional apparatus of government seems to be another major dimension of regime support, empirically distinguishable from generalized "agreement on fundamentals." Citizens are apparently able to dislike something or other about the actions of government and at the same time support its continuation institutionally unchanged, and their levels of support in this respect apparently fluctuate over time. An instructive example is the differences in French responses to identical questions put at different times concerning which political regimes seemed to be functioning better or worse than the French regime. From January 1958 to January 1965, the percentage saying each country named worked better than the French dropped in every case and the percentage saying the French regime worked better increased in every case.[64] Again, although 41 percent of a sample in a small Midwestern American city said, in 1966, that there were things Congress had done which they did not like (about some of which they claimed to feel strongly), only 20 percent of them thought any proposals for changing Congress should be given serious attention; although 44 percent said the city council had done something they particularly disliked, and only 20 percent thought the council was doing a good or excellent job, less than a third thought the form of government should be changed.[65] This perspective also leads us to view not as deviant, undemocratic views, but as probable indicators of probably normal regime support, the fact that more Americans think the majority of people usually *in*correct in their ideas on important questions (42 percent) than think the majority correct (38 percent), or that Congress is thought more correct than "the people" in its "views on broad national issues" (42 percent as against 38 percent).[66] Similarly, it becomes understandable why, when only half the American public thinks it makes much difference at all which party wins the election, some two-thirds to three-fourths of them make a point of voting at all elections, whether or not they have any specific interest in them,[67] and almost nine-tenths of them (87 percent) think having elections makes government pay some or a good deal of attention to what the people think.[68] Although Almond and Verba consider such indicators as these under the heading of "input affect," meaning essentially demand-input ("the feelings people have both about those agencies and processes that are involved in the election of public officials, and about the enactment of public policies"[69]), they seem much more intelligible viewed under the heading of regime support, i.e., support for the apparatus of government in general.

Our information about regime support phenomena, then, is no more adequate or satisfactory than our information about support for the political community. What there is of it, however, does seem to indicate that symbolic satisfaction with the process of government is probably more important than specific, instrumental satisfaction with the policy output of the process. Thus Thomas Anton has noticed, concerning the budget process, that "it is not the document which creates satisfaction, but the process of putting it together. . . . [The] budget, as document and process, creates symbolic satisfaction built upon the idea that affairs of state are being dealt with, that responsibility is being exercised, and that rationality prevails."[70] Dye's conclusion, after studying a voluminous array of the content of policy outputs, was that "The *way* in which a society authoritatively allocates values may be an even more important question than the outcomes of these value allocations. Our commitments to democratic processes are essentially commitments to a mode of decision-making. The legitimacy of the democratic form of government has never really depended upon the policy outcomes which it is expected to produce."[71] And deGrazia has said, more poetically, "The whole *process* of representation becomes an acting out of a play in which the actors are independent within the limits of the state, the setting, and the changing tastes of the audience. Their role is meaningful but it has no direct connection with the ticket the audience files for admission."[72]

Whereas political research has by and large neglected to study support for the political community and the political regime, it has paid considerable attention to support for "political authorities." Elections, of course, are considered an indispensable feature of representative government by anybody's definition, and election results in representative systems are almost universally interpreted as indices of support for incumbent authorities. The innumerable public opinion polls between elections which ask the level of voters' satisfaction or dissatisfaction with the ruling government's performance in general, with the performance of various individual officeholders or agencies, or with the handling of particular problems are likewise taken as indicators of the rising and falling level of support for authorities.

No doubt such data are properly interpreted as measures of such support. But the question is, what should be read into them beyond that simple indication? "Democracy," says Schumpeter, "means only that the people have the opportunity of accepting or refusing the men who are to rule them."[73] Our earlier discussion of the role of issues and policies in elections cautions us not to assume hastily that voters are voting up one set of policies and voting down another when they go to the polls.[74] A unique series of data about British opinion in 1966 strongly intimates that we ought not even assume that they are voting up one set of officeholders and voting down another in quite the simple, straightforward, preferential fashion we have always taken for granted. The data shown in Figure 1 clearly demonstrate that, at least in Britain in 1966, many voters seem to be giving or withdrawing support from the whole apparatus of government officialdom and not, as one might at first think, transferring support from one set of authorities to another. To a remarkable degree, support for Government goes up as support for Opposition goes up, and support for Opposition goes down as support for Government goes down. One is strongly tempted to conclude, though it may be premature, that the support for authorities is much more closely related to regime support and much less related to individual voter preferences for individual authority figures than anyone has hitherto suspected.[75]

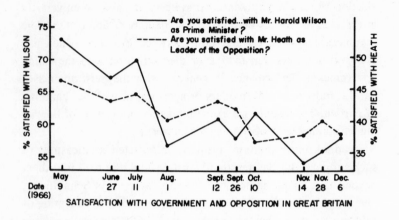

SATISFACTION WITH GOVERNMENT AND OPPOSITION IN GREAT BRITAIN

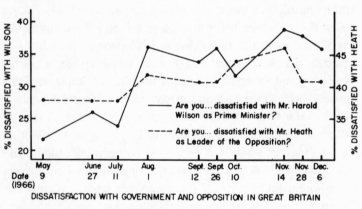

DISSATISFACTION WITH GOVERNMENT AND OPPOSITION IN GREAT BRITAIN

Source POLLS II (4), p. 44 (Sum.'67)

FIGURE 1. Trends in Support for British Government and Opposition Leaders, 1966

CONCLUSION

The conceptualization of support sketched out here is only that. It is not a theory, or even a few hypotheses. Indeed, it is not even a very complete conceptualization, since many important questions are left open—how do we visualize support in a complex, multilevel, pluralistic government? What is the connection between support for local as against national (and, in federal systems, intermediate) authorities, regime, and political community? Between support for different segments of the regime at different levels? What is the relevance of the notion to supranational and intergovernmental politics?

What bearing has all this on representative government? Surely it does not suggest that to maintain representative democracy is more difficult or that representative democracy is less desirable just because it might seem to depend less on support deriving from mechanically satisfying demand-inputs than it does on the generation of support through quite different mechanisms. The question still is, how do representative bodies contribute to the generation and maintenance of support? In what respects and for what particular aspects of the task are they superior to nonrepresentative institutions? These are questions to be answered by empirical research.

NOTES

1. The best analytical surveys of representation theory are those of A. H. Birch, *Representative and Responsible Government* (Toronto: University of Toronto Press, 1964), and Alfred de Grazia, *Public and Republic* (New York: Knopf, 1951).
2. Bryce's views are expressed, for example, in *Modern Democracies* (New York: Macmillan, 1921), vol. II, 335–357, reprinted above, pp. 21–32. Lippmann's can be found in *Public Opinion* (New York: Penguin Books, 1946), especially pp. 216–220. While General de Gaulle has, of course, not contributed formally to literature of

this kind, Gaullist views are well known from various speeches, debates, and publications preceding the creation of the Fifth French Republic. They are conveniently discussed in Roy C. Macridis and Bernard E. Brown, *The de Gaulle Republic* (Homewood, Ill.: Dorsey Press, 1960), pp. 124–131.

3. Joseph P. Clark, *Congress: The Sapless Branch* (New York: Harper & Row, 1964); *The Senate Establishment* (New York: Hill & Wang, 1964).

4. Gerhard Loewenberg, *Parliament in the German Political System* (Ithaca, N.Y.: Cornell University Press, 1967), p. 1.

5. Heinz Eulau, "Changing Views of Representation," in Ithiel de Sola Pool, ed., *Contemporary Political Science: Toward Empirical Theory* (New York: McGraw-Hill, 1967), p. 55.

6. Julius Turner, *Party and Constituency: Pressures on Congress,* Johns Hopkins University Studies in Historical and Political Science, 69: 1 (Baltimore, Md.: Johns Hopkins University Press, 1952), 178. Italics added.

7. Gabriel A. Almond and Sidney Verba, *The Civic Culture* (Princeton, N.J.: Princeton University Press, 1963), p. 214. More recently, Almond has specifically identified this kind of model as a sort of paradigm for developed representative political systems, listing "responsiveness" (to demand inputs) as a capability of the most developed political systems. Gabriel A. Almond, "A Developmental Approach to Political Systems," *World Politics,* 17 (1965), 183–214, especially pp. 197 ff.

8. See, for example, the familiar discussion in Bernard R. Berelson, Paul F. Lazarsfeld, and William N. McPhee, *Voting* (Chicago: University of Chicago Press, 1954), pp. 305–323. The particular propositions listed here are supported, in every instance, by survey data from various political systems collected at various different times. Although systematically analyzed in the original research for this paper, the data are not reported here because of limitations of space. The more relevant compilations and commentaries include the following: Hadley Cantril, *The Pattern of Human Concerns* (New Brunswick, N.J.: Rutgers University Press, 1965), pp. 167–171; Hadley Cantril and Mildred Strunk, *Public Opinion 1935–46* (Princeton, N.J.: Princeton University Press, 1951); Angus Campbell, Philip E. Converse, Warren E. Miller, and Donald E. Stokes, *The American Voter* (New York: John Wiley, 1960); Philip E. Converse and George Dupeux, "Politicization of the Electorate in France and the United States," reprinted from *Public Opinion Quarterly,* XXVI (1962), in Angus Campbell, et al., *Elections and the Political Order* (New York: John Wiley, 1966), pp. 269–291; Philip E. Converse, "New Dimensions of Meaning for Cross-Section Sample Surveys in Politics," *International Social Science Journal,* XVI: 1 (1964), 19–34; Raymond A. Bauer, Ithiel de Sola Pool, and Lewis Anthony Dexter, *American Business and Public Policy* (New York: Atherton Press, 1963); Donald E. Stokes, "Spatial Models of Party Competition," reprinted from *American Political Science Review,* LVII (1963), in Angus Campbell, et al., *Elections* and the *Political Order* (New York: John Wiley, 1966), pp. 161–179; Robert Axelrod, "The Structure of Public Opinion on Policy

Issues," *Public Opinion Quarterly*, XXXI: 1 (Spring 1967), 51–60; Elisabeth Noelle and Erich Peter Neumann, eds., *Jahrbuch für öffentliche Meinung, III (1958–1964)*, (Allensbach and Bonn: Verlag für Demoskopie, 1965); William N. McPhee and William A. Glaser, ed., *Public Opinion and Congressional Elections* (New York: The Free Press, 1962); Leon D. Epstein, "Electoral Decision and Policy Mandate: An Empirical Example," *Public Opinion Quarterly*, XXVIII (1964), 564–572; and William Buchanan, "An Inquiry into Purposive Voting," *Journal of Politics*, 18 (1965), 281–296.

9. Donald E. Stokes and Warren E. Miller, "Party Government and the Saliency of Congress," *Public Opinion Quarterly*, XXVI (1962), 531–546, reprinted in Campbell, et al., *Elections and the Political Order*, pp. 194–211.

10. Committee on Political Parties of the American Political Science Association, "Toward a More Responsible Two-Party System," Supplement, *The American Political Science Review* (September 1950).

11. Morris Showell, "Political Consciousness and Attitudes in the State of Washington," *Public Opinion Quarterly*, XVII (Fall 1953), 394–400.

12. University of Michigan Survey Research Center Study 0504, Preliminary Code Book, 1967, Deck 02, Columns 51, 52. I am grateful to Professor Warren E. Miller and the Inter-University Consortium for Political Research for their permission to cite this and other preliminary marginal tabulations.

13. Stokes and Miller, "Party Government and the Saliency of Congress, p. 209.

14. Philip E. Converse, "The Nature of Belief Systems in Mass Publics," in David E. Apter, ed., *Ideology and Discontent* (New York: The Free Press, 1964), pp. 206–261.

15. Mark Abrams, "Social Trends and Electoral Behavior," reprinted from *British Journal of Sociology*, XIII (1962), 228–242 in Richard Rose, ed., *Studies in British Politics* (New York: St. Martin's Press, 1966), p. 136.

16. Campbell, et al., *Elections and the Political Order*, especially pp. 68–75.

17. *Ibid.*, p. 169

18. Werner Zolnhöfer, "Parteiidentifizierung in der Bundesrepublik und den Vereinigten Staaten," in Erwin K. Scheuch and Rudolf Wildenman, eds., *Zur Soziologie der Wahl*, Sonderheft 9/1965, *Kölner Zeitschrift für Soziologie und Sozialpsychologie* (Cologne and Opladen: Westdeutscher Verlag, 1965), pp. 126–168.

19. R. S. Milne and H. C. MacKenzie, "The Floating Vote," reprinted from *Political Studies*, III (1955), 65–68, in Richard Rose, ed., *Studies in British Politics* (New York: St. Martin's Press, 1966), pp. 145–149, quote from p. 145.

20. Floyd Hunter, *Community Power Structure* (Chapel Hill, N. C.: University of North Carolina Press, 1953). For a general commentary on this line of studies see Nelson W. Polsby, *Community Power and Political Theory* (New Haven, Conn.: Yale University Press, 1963).

21. Robert A. Dahl, *A Preface to Democratic Theory* (Chicago: University of Chicago Press, 1956), especially chap. 3; *Who Governs* (New Haven, Conn.: Yale University Press, 1961).

22. Such problems are discussed in "Electoral Studies and Democratic Theory: I. A British View," by John Plamenatz, and II. "A Continental View," by Giovanni Sartori, *Political Studies,* VI (1958), 1–15; Jack Walker, "A Critique of the Elitist Theory of Democracy," *American Political Science Review,* LX (1966), 285–295, and the reply by Robert A. Dahl, "Further Reflections on 'The Elitist Theory of Democracy,'" *ibid.,* pp. 296–304; and Peter Bachrach, *The Theory of Democratic Elitism: A Critique* (Boston: Little, Brown, 1967).

23. Sidney Verba, et al., "Public Opinion and the War in Vietnam," *American Political Science Review,* LXI (1967), 317–333, especially p. 318.

24. Converse and Dupeux, "Politicization of the Electorate," p. 291.

25. Earl Latham, *The Group Basis of Politics* (Ithaca, N.Y.: Cornell University Press, 1952), p. 35.

26. John C. Wahlke, Heinz Eulau, William Buchanan, and Leroy C. Ferguson, *The Legislative System* (New York: John Wiley, 1962), pp. 267–286; Warren E. Miller and Donald E. Stokes, "Constituency Influence in Congress," *American Political Science Review,* LVII (1963), 45–56, reprinted in Campbell, et al., *Elections and the Political Order,* pp. 351–372; and Donald E. Stokes, "A Variance Components Model of Political Effects," in John Claunch, ed., *Mathematical Applications in Political Science* (Dallas, Texas: The Arnold Foundation of Southern Methodist University, 1965), p. 62.

27. Malcolm E. Jewell and Samuel C. Patterson, *The Legislative Process in the United States* (New York: Random House, 1966), pp. 351–352.

28. Warren E. Miller and Donald E. Stokes, "Constituency Influence in Congress," p. 368.

29. John W. Kingdon, "Politicians' Beliefs about Voters," *American Political Science Review,* LXI (1967), 137–145, especially p. 144.

30. Warren E. Miller and Donald E. Stokes, "Constituency Influence in Congress"; Charles F. Cnudde and Donald J. McCrone, "The Linkage between Constituency Attitudes and Congressional Voting Behavior: A Casual Model," *American Political Science Review,* LX (1966), 66–72.

31. David Easton, *A Framework for Political Analysis* (Englewood Cliffs, N. J.: Prentice-Hall, 1965), p. 126; *A Systems Analysis of Political Life* (New York: John Wiley, 1965), pp. 353 ff.

32. Wahlke, Eulau, Buchanan, and Ferguson, *The Legislative System,* p. 25.

33. Lewis A. Froman, Jr., "An Analysis of Public Policies in Cities," *Journal of Politics,* 29 (1967), 95.

34. Thomas R. Dye, *Politics, Economics and the Public: Policy Outcomes in the American States* (Chicago: Rand McNally, 1966), p. 293.

35. Philips Cutright, "Political Structure, Economic Development, and National Security Programs," *American Journal of Sociology,* LXX (1965), 537–548.

36. David H. Blake, "Leadership Succession and Its Effects on Foreign Policy as Observed in the General Assembly," mimeographed paper prepared for the Annual Meeting of the Midwest Conference of Political Scientists, West Lafayette, Indiana, April 27–29, 1967.

37. Eugene J. Meehan, *Contemporary Political Thought* (Homewood, Ill.: The Dorsey Press, 1967), p. 180.

38. Easton describes this distinction as that between "a stream of activities flowing from the authorities in a system" (outputs) and "the infinite chain of effects that might flow from an authoritative allocation" (outcomes). *A Systems Analysis of Political Life,* pp. 349, 351.

39. Leon Lindberg, "The Role of the European Parliament in an Emerging European Community," in Elke Frank, ed., *Lawmakers in a Changing World* (Englewood Cliffs, N.J.: Prentice-Hall, 1966), p. 108. The same point has been made in John Wahlke, "Behavioral Analyses of Representative Bodies," in Austin Ranney, ed., *Essays in the Behavioral Study of Politics* (Urbana: University of Illinois Press, 1962), pp. 173–190, and is indirectly made by Malcolm E. Jewell and Samuel C. Patterson, *The Legislative Process in the United States* (New York: Random House, 1966), pp. 528–531.

40. Bertrand de Jouvenel, "On the Nature of Political Science," *American Political Science Review,* LV (1961), 777.

41. Easton, *A Systems Analysis of Political Life,* p. 268.

42. *Ibid.,* pp. 272, 273. Easton himself later (434n.) makes the much stronger assertion still that, "Under some circumstances the need for outputs to bolster support may be reduced to the vanishing point."

43. *Ibid.,* p. 273.

44. Murray Edelman, *The Symbolic Uses of Politics* (Urbana: University of Illinois Press, 1964).

45. Thomas J. Anton, "Roles and Symbols in the Determination of State Expenditures," *Midwest Journal of Political Science,* XI (1967), 27–43, especially p. 39.

46. Alfred de Grazia, *Public and Republic,* p. 170.

47. T. V. Smith, "Two Functions of the American State Legislator," *Annals of the American Academy of Political and Social Science,* 195 (1938), 187.

48. Heinz Eulau and Katherine Hinckley, "Legislative Institutions and Processes," in James A. Robinson, ed., *Political Science Annual,* 1 (1966), 85–189, especially pp. 85–86.

49. Samuel H. Beer, "The British Legislature and the Problem of Mobilizing Consent," in Elke Frank, *Lawmakers,* p. 31.

50. Samuel C. Patterson, *Midwest Legislative Politics* (Mid-America Assembly on State Legislatures, Participants' Edition, 1966), p. 114.

51. David B. Truman, "The Representative Function in Western Systems," in Edward H. Buehrig, ed., *Essays in Political Science* (Bloomington: Indiana University Press, 1966), pp. 84–96, especially 90.

52. "Political community" refers to "some minimal readiness or ability (of a group of people) to continue working together to solve their political problems" (*A Systems Analysis of Political Life,* p. 172). "Political regime" refers to the values and principles, norms ("op-

erating rules and rules of the game") and structures of authority (authority-*roles*) by which, over a period of time authoritative decisions are made in the political community (*ibid.*, pp. 190–211). Political authorities are the persons who occupy the authoritative roles at any given point in time (*ibid.*, pp. 212–219).

53. *Ibid.*, p. 332.
54. Key, *Public Opinion and American Democracy* (New York: Knopf, 1961), p. 549.
55. Almond and Verba, *The Civic Culture*, pp. 101–105.
56. *Ibid.*, p. 551.
57. The "participant" is "an active participant in the political input process," the "subject" hardly at all oriented toward input objects but positively (if passively) oriented affectively "toward the output, administrative, or 'downward flow' side of the political system," and the "parochial" detached from political roles of every sort, on both input and output sides. Almond and Verba, *The Civic Culture*, pp. 161, 19, 17 respectively.
58. *Ibid.*, p. 143.
59. Peter Bachrach, p. 38.
60. Julian L. Woodward and Elmo Roper, "The Political Activity of American Citizens," *American Political Science Review*, XLIV (1950), 872–885.
61. OMGUS, October 26, December 13, 1945; January 31, June 7, August 9, September 3, 1946. Reported in Cantril and Strunk, *Public Opinion*, pp. 582–583.
62. Noelle and Neumann, *Jahrbuch* (July 1958), 265.
63. Key's discussion (*Public Opinion*, pp. 30 ff.) of "supportive," "permissive," "negative," and "decisional" consensus is most instructive here. See also Herbert McClosky, "Consensus and Ideology in American Politics," *American Political Science Review*, LVIII (1964), 361–382, and James W. Prothro and Charles W. Grigg, "Fundamental Principles of Democracy: Bases of Agreement and Disagreement," *Journal of Politics*, 22 (1960), 276–294.
64. Drop in percent saying other regime better than France, 25 percent for G.B.; 28 percent for U.S.A.; 7 percent for Italy; 31 percent for West Germany; 16 percent for U.S.S.R. Increase in percent saying French worked better: 15 percent for G.B.; 13 percent for U.S.A.; 1 percent for Italy; 14 percent for West Germany; 9 percent for U.S.S.R. (*Sondages*, 26: 1 [1966]).
65. Iowa City Form of Government Study, 1966, Code Book. University of Iowa Laboratory for Political Research.
66. A.I.P.O. July 17, 1939, and August 8, 1939, reported in Hazel Erskine, "The Polls," *Public Opinion Quarterly*, various issues. The remainder of responses in each instance were DK and NA.
67. Forty-nine percent and 51 percent in two separate polls in September 1946, for example. A.I.P.O. reported in Erskine.
68. Survey Research Center, 1966, SRC Study 0504, ICPR Preliminary Code Book.
69. Almond and Verba, *The Civic Culture*, p. 101.
70. Anton, "Roles and Symbols," pp. 39–40.
71. Dye, *Politics, Economics and the Public*, p. 300.
72. De Grazia, *Public and Republic*, p. 170. Italics not in original.

73. Joseph A. Schumpeter, *Capitalism, Socialism, and Democracy* (New York: Harper & Brothers, 1947), p. 285.
74. See above, pp. 143–148.
75. For a summary of the implications of available studies on the dynamics of support and suggestions for further cross-national study of the problem see G. R. Boynton, Samuel C. Patterson, and John C. Wahlke, "Dimensions of Support in Legislative Systems," in Allan Kornberg, ed., *Legislatures in Comparative Perspective* (New York: McKay, 1971).

For Further Reading

Butt, Ronald. *The Power of Parliament*. London: Constable, 1967.

Crick, Bernard. *The Reform of Parliament*. New York: Anchor Books, 1965.

Debuyst, Frederic. *La Fonction Parlementaire en Belgique*. Brussels: Centre de Recherche et d'Information Socio-Politiques, 1967.

DiRenzo, Gordon J. *Personality, Power and Politics: A Social Psychological Analysis of the Italian Deputy and His Parliamentary System*. Notre Dame: University of Notre Dame Press, 1967.

Frank, Elke, ed. *Lawmakers in a Changing World*. New York: Prentice-Hall, 1966.

Gerlich, Peter, and Kramer, Helmut. *Abgeordnete in der Parteiendemokratie*. Vienna: Verlag für Geschichte und Politik, 1969. (An empirical study of the Vienna City Council).

Hirsch, Herbert, and Hancock, M. Donald. *Comparative Legislative Systems: A Reader in Theory and Research*. New York: The Free Press, 1971.

Jewell, Malcolm E., and Patterson, Samuel C. *The Legislative Process in the United States*. New York: Random House, 1966.

Kornberg, Allan. *Canadian Legislative Behavior: A Study of the 25th Parliament*. New York: Holt, Rinehart and Winston, 1967.

Kornberg, Allan, ed. *Legislatures in Comparative Perspective*. New York: McKay, 1971.

Kornberg, Allan, and Musolf, Lloyd D., eds., *Legislatures in Developmental Perspective*. Durham, N.C.: Duke University Press, 1970.

Loewenberg, Gerhard. *Parliament in the German Political System*. Ithaca, N. Y.: Cornell University Press, 1967.

MacRae, Duncan. *Parliament, Parties, and Society in France, 1946–1958*. New York: St. Martin's Press, 1967.

172

Marongiu, Antonio. *Medieval Parliaments. A Comparative Study.* London: Eyre & Spottiswoode, 1968.

Matthews, Donald R. *U.S. Senators and Their World.* New York: Vintage Books, originally published, 1960.

Meynaud, Jean, ed. "The Parliamentary Profession," *International Social Science Journal,* XIII (1961).

Morris-Jones, W. H. *Parliament in India.* Philadelphia: University of Pennsylvania Press, 1957.

Patterson, Samuel C. "Comparative Legislative Behavior: A Review Essay", *Midwest Journal of Political Science,* XII (1968), 599–616.

Patterson, Samuel C., and Wahlke, John C., eds. *Comparative Legislative Behavior: Frontiers of Research.* New York: John Wiley, 1972.

Wahlke, John C., Eulau, Heinz, Buchanan, William, and Ferguson, Leroy C. *The Legislative System.* New York: John Wiley, 1962.

Wheare, K. C. *Legislatures.* New York: Oxford University Press, 1963.

Williams, Philip M. *The French Parliament. Politics in the Fifth Republic.* New York: Frederick A. Praeger, 1968.